D1461751

800 549 198

THE BEATLES

Messages from John, Paul, George and Ringo

By their friend CHRIS HUTCHINS

(Or CRISPY HUTCH as they called him)

Neville Ness House

Published in Great Britain in 2015 by

Neville Ness House Ltd

www.chrishutchins.info nevillenesshouse@sky.com

Copyright © Chris Hutchins 2015

ISBN: 978-0-9933566-0-5

A CIP catalogue record for this book is available from the British Library.

Cover design and art work by Carlos & Numa (www.numarta.com)

ABOUT THE AUTHOR

CHRIS HUTCHINS is an established author of highly acclaimed biographies of the rich, the famous and the royals. His first, **FERGIE CONFIDENTIAL**, was an intimate biography of the Duchess of York and chronicled her troubled marriage to the Queen's favourite son. This was followed by a revelatory biography of the late Princess of Wales, **DIANA'S NIGHTMARE: The Family**, and an acclaimed psychological profile of her, **DIANA ON THE EDGE. ATHINA: The Last Onassis** penetrated deeply into the world of the Onassis dynasty. More recently Hutchins turned his attention to matters Russian with fearless biographies of that country's leader, **PUTIN**, and best-known oligarch **ABRAMOVICH: The billionaire from nowhere**. The author recently returned to the royal stage with **HARRY: The People's Prince**.

CONTENTS

A POSTCARD FROM JOHN

IT was a warm June day in 1965 when the postcard landed on the desk of my office at the NME (New Musical Express), deep in the heart of Covent Garden. The card was addressed to me but John, whose unmistakable handwriting marked him out as my correspondent, began it 'Dear Mick', clearly alluding to Mick Jagger (more on that later). The message went on in typical Lennon vein: 'Woke up this mornin' – cornflakes – brown sugar – dig? Shoes – mac – raining down – still digging? … Folk fingers – brass coffee – couldn't sleep – broke my line. Won't be back in time. DIG???' He signed it 'The BIFOLKALS'.

I read it over and over again but never could work out half of what he was trying to say. Except, that is, for the 'brown sugar' bit. It was the term in those days – and this was the Sixties, remember – for heroin (and more on that follows too).

But it was the picture on the other side that was most interesting – a photograph of himself, Paul, George and Ringo. Over each face he had inked-in dark glasses and on his one hand showing, a black glove. There was more: in the centre of the group he had drawn in a fifth person, a fifth Beatle and it was none other than the late Stuart Sutcliffe. Stuart had always worn dark glasses.

The card had been sent from Genoa mid-way through the Beatles' Italian tour. John had phoned before they left to remind me that I had promised to try to set up a meeting with Elvis Presley for him that summer. But the conversation had become maudlin when I reminded him that he was going to talk to me for an article about Stuart. Sutcliffe was the group's original bass player and, inspired by the Crickets, he was also the man who came up with their name – The Beatles.

But to John he was much more – he was the best friend he'd ever had, ever would have.

Sutcliffe had died of a brain haemorrhage in Hamburg in April 1962. The injury was caused by a beating he took after a Beatles gig the previous year. He was a brilliant artist but not a particularly good musician. It was Lennon who persuaded him to buy a bass guitar and join the group as a founder member so they could be together.

When he died John was devastated. He wept for days and (according to Yoko Ono) he said of him years later, 'Stu was my alter ego, a spirit in my world, a guiding force.'

In that sad telephone chat before they set off for Milan, I asked him if he was happy: 'I'd be a lot happier if Stuart was still part of us,' he said 'The Beatles would be complete.' And before he rang off he said 'I'll send you something.'

The postcard arrived a few days later. I have placed it on the cover of this book as John's tribute to his dearest friend, the man who helped him found the Beatles.

CHRIS HUTCHINS

1

PARIS

THE postcard I received from Genoa was not the first John sent me from foreign parts. In January 1964, he dispatched one from Paris where I had left him, Paul, George and Ringo just a few days earlier. The only sign of Lennon using artistic license on that one was a flag he had drawn with the letter 'B' on it flying above a photograph of the George V hotel where they were staying.

We'd had something of a wild time in Paris where they were appearing at the city's hallowed Olympia, playing on a bill topped by local heartthrob Johnny Hallyday – a bit of a tense coupling because, the Frenchman told them, that before they got famous he had refused to have them as his backing group.

The George V was the swankiest hotel in the French capital and I am not sure the management approved of the comings-and-goings that went on during the celebrations in their suite that followed their first triumphant night at the Olympia. John had invited a number of people neither he nor any of the others had ever met before 'to party' in their suite. A lot of very expensive alcohol was consumed and the subsequent bill far exceeded their earnings for the weeklong gig.

My lasting memory of the Paris adventure is of what occurred the following morning. I had arrived in the suite to find Paul – the most moderate drinker in the band – already up and, draped in one of the hotel's finest white fluffy robes, was seated at the piano he had asked to be installed for their stay. We exchanged greetings before I sunk into a sofa to listen to him play, humming along as he did so. There was a knock at the door and I responded to Paul's request to answer it believing it to be the coffee we had ordered to cure our, er, 'headaches'.

Alas, it was not the coffee. The new arrival was Dick James, the Beatles genial music publisher and the man best known at that time as the singer of the eponymous Robin Hood TV theme. Seeing Paul seated at the piano he got straight down to business: 'Mornin', mornin'. Glad to see you're at work already. Got some new songs for me?'

Paul turned and gave him a slightly nervous look: 'See what you think of this, Dick. I'm still working on it mind.'

And with that he played a few chords and sang the few lines he had worked out of what was clearly a plaintive ballad. Dick James seemed especially thoughtful as he and I sat listening in silence. Paul struck a final chord and turned around to ask 'How's that?'

The publisher's reaction was not enthusiastic. After a sustained pause he finally said 'That's sweet, very sweet, but have you got anything with "Yeah, yeah, yeah" in it?'

McCartney looked devastated. The song he had just given us an exclusive preview of was *Yesterday*.

Yesterday is the most covered song in history. At the last count 3,700 artistes had recorded it and the song was the most played ever on American radio.

2

HAMBURG

AT Massey & Coggins – the Liverpool electrical firm where he landed his first job, winding coils – they nicknamed Paul 'Mantovani McCartney' after the well-known classical conductor because of his long hair. Ringo, a favourite target for local bullies, got badly beaten up as he walked home one night from the Admiral Grove pub in the Dingle district of his home city because he wouldn't give them the shilling (5p) each demanded. On the road George became depressed when he felt the others were pushing him into the background. John used to cry himself to sleep when his thoughts turned to the mother who had abandoned him.

All of that is gleaned from the notebooks I wrote in endlessly during my first days (well, mostly nights) with the Beatles at the back of the Star Club, a dive of a club in the Grosse Freiheit off Hamburg's notorious Reeperbahn in 1962. I was there as a temporary roadie for Little Richard (it's a long story, but I'll come to it) and the 'Fab Four', as the legendary American rocker named them, were working their passage in the music business.

It was a shaky start (John didn't trust 'reporters') but we got on well once we discovered we had two things in common: all five of us were crazy about rock'n'roll – and we were hungry. Little Richard's fat salary solved the latter problem – we ate in his dressing room and he charged the food to the club owner, Manfred Weissleder.

We were of similar age – two of them were older than me, two younger (John and Ringo were born in 1940, Paul in 1942, George in 1943 and me in 1941). Oh yes, and we all took 'uppers', amphetamines which loosened tongues particularly when washed down with strong German beer.

The main topic of conversation on the first day was … the Beatles. 'Our manager Brian Epstein says we're going to be bigger than Elvis,' snapped John. 'So one day you'll have to queue up with the rest for an interview with us.'

That day had not arrived, however, and I went through the familiar ritual of asking them about their musical aspirations. Who was their greatest influence? 'Little Richard,' said Ringo aware that the singer was within earshot, 'Chuck Berry,' said

George. 'Elvis,' said Paul. 'Yeah, before Elvis there was nothing. He's the King,' said John in a quote that was to be re-published many, many times over the years, although it was actually a barb aimed at Richard whose shrill response was '*Ah*, am the King of rock'n'roll. *Ah* was singing rock before anybody knew what rock was. Sure Elvis was one of the builders, but Ah was the architect.'

'Sure thing, grandfather,' said John whom I was later to refer to in print as 'The Beatle that bit'. When he had an audience – even if was only his fellow band members and me – he had to perform. In reality, he was highly respectful of the American legend and had earlier asked him for an autograph. He showed me the one he got. It read 'To John. May God bless you always, Little Richard, 1710 Virginia Road, Los Angeles, California.' It was something he treasured although in later years he was to question the sanity of those who collect stars' signatures.

Much of the conversation in those heady nights was about things back home. John sent his Star Club earnings back to Liverpool for Cynthia (who, he told me, he had married the that summer and who was expecting their son, Julian, though he was under strict instructions from manager Epstein to keep both facts secret: 'Fans don't like stars who are unavailable, John.'). He survived on what he could earn by moonlighting between Beatles sets at nearby clubs where he played for the strippers: 'I love talking to the prossies (prostitutes). They're honest. They've got nothing to hide.'

Being honest himself, he also admitted that he had a Hamburg girlfriend: Bettina, a buxom barmaid who kept him in drink and pills and could be relied upon to call out for her favourite numbers when the Beatles were on stage.

The topic inspired Ringo to deliver the message about one of his most disastrous dates: 'I turned up in me best gear – a real Ted suit complete with crepe sole shoes. I thought I was going to knock her dead with that lot! Anyway, we took the bus to a cinema, walked into the foyer and I bought the tickets. She started heading upstairs where the best seats were. But I took her arm and led her down to the stalls where the only two seats left were right in the front row. It was as much as I could afford, you see. We sat there for three hours with our necks achings. Funny I never saw her again ...

I heard him repeat the story almost word for word a few nights later when Richard and his keyboard player Billy Preston invited us back to his hotel suite 'for supper'. Alas, the supper turned out to be some dried-up sandwiches and our hosts had other ideas about how to entertain us. In a bid to emphasise our heterosexuality, Ringo told the story of his date and I talked about the girl I was going to marry. In a lull between anecdotes, the pair of us made a dash for the door and returned to the relative safety of the Grosse Freiheit. Lucky escape.

'That's one little adventure I won't be telling Harry and Elsie about,' he said, referring to his parents as he always did by their first names.

I had accompanied Richard to Hamburg at the request of the promoter Don Arden after losing my job at the NME. Arden – Sharon Osbourne's father, incidentally – had asked me to set up a rival music paper which he wanted to call The Enemy because he hated the NME's owner Maurice Kinn. When Mr Kinn heard about it he gave me my marching orders. Alas, Arden failed to raise the money for his planned paper and, temporarily out of work; I accepted the two-week job as Richard's minder for the German engagement.

Paul talked about how his employment at the firm – the one where they called him Mantovani – came to an end. 'I was hopeless [at the job]. Everybody else would wind fourteen coils a day while I'd get through one and a half – and mine were the ones that never worked. After a bit I started getting lunchtime dates playing at the Cavern. I had to whip out of work over the back wall at lunchtime and go in the next day and say I'd been ill. One day I just didn't get back and that was that.' Paul's message was that had he been any good at the job one of the most famed musicians of all time might today be a retired coil winder.

Wherever he went Paul, the strolling minstrel, said he composed songs in his head. 'I used to walk home if I didn't have enough for the bus fare, but I never minded that. I wrote lots of songs on those walks home: *World Without Love* and *Love of the Love* included, though John helped me polish them up. I used to go to his house and I remember those walks home very well. I had to cross this horrible pitch-black golf course. I'd always be singing, but if ever I came across someone in the dark, I'd shut up and try to pretend it hadn't been me. Met a copper like that once. I had a guitar round my neck and was quite cheerfully playing and singing at the top of my voice. I thought he was going to arrest me, but he walked up and asked if I'd give him guitar lessons.'

All four came from similar backgrounds although George was anxious to point out that John was the only one who was raised in a privately owned house (his Aunt Mimi's) whereas he, Paul and Ringo all lived in council houses. Ringo, who had spent more than three of his childhood years in hospital suffering from peritonitis and pleurisy, was the worst off. His job paid just over £2 a week of which he had to pay all but fifteen shillings (75p) over to Elsie for his keep, which is probably why he was reluctant to hand the Admiral Grove bullies the cash they needed for the pub.

With the seemingly endless pill-popping going on it was inevitable that the subject of drugs would arise. John was fascinated by what effects could be achieved by trying substances other than the moderate 'speed' pills which Bettina came up with. A German friend addicted to heroin had told him of the dream-like status the drug induced: 'Just think of the songs we could write on that,' he said. 'They say it brings back vivid memories.'

At that stage, however, 'prellies' (the appetite suppressant drug Preludin then freely available in Germany) and Benzedrine, supplied by the Star Club waiters, was all they needed to stay awake until (and often long after) dawn.

Inevitably, discussions about music always came round to the mention of one man: Elvis Presley. John said he was just 15 when Elvis's first British hit, *Heartbreak Hotel*, entered the charts. He heard it on Radio Luxembourg and the song, about the feelings of loneliness followed by the break-up of a relationship, struck a chord with him. But it was the voice of this mysterious stranger, just five years his senior, which had a devastating effect on him.

'When I saw pictures of him I tried to copy the way he looked. I did my best to copy his hairstyle by growing long sideboards, shrunk my jeans and did everything I could to look mean and moody. [Aunt] Mimi says I changed overnight. I had this poster of him in my bedroom and nothing else mattered. I left everything everywhere. Rock'n'roll had taken over and Elvis, according to Mimi, was the culprit.'

From an earlier conversation Paul remembered that I had mentioned striking up a telephone acquaintance with Elvis's manager 'Colonel' Tom Parker. Using the office phone during my early *NME* days, I had called his office in the Hollywood studios operated by Paramount Pictures, night after night (morning/afternoon in LA). On one occasion I got lucky: all the guys who had rebuffed my earlier attempts to speak to him had left the office and Parker himself picked up the phone to answer my incoming call. 'Is your call paid?' were the first words he uttered to me. It was, and he gave me an interview. He subsequently liked what I wrote and thereafter I phoned him for news of Elvis on a regular basis. As a cub reporter on the paper I had struck gold by forming a fledgling friendship with the most important manager in the music business – one who had previously made it a rule 'never to talk to the Press'.

'Do you think you could ever get us to meet Elvis?' asked John.

I said I would try but I had to meet him first.

None of us could have imagined what a train reaction of events that seemingly innocent conversation between five ardent rock'n'roll fans was to set off in the years that followed. It's all going to come out here.

'This was the point of our lives [Hamburg] when we found pills, uppers. That's the only way we could continue playing for so long. They were called Preludin, and you could buy them over the counter. We never thought we were doing anything wrong, but we'd get really wired and go on for days. So with beer and Preludin, that's how we survived' - Ringo Starr

3

BEATLEMANIA IS BORN

THE night of 18 April 1963 was memorable for two reasons. It marked the birth of Beatlemania and Paul met the girl of his dreams.

But let me catch up: the Beatles had returned from Germany and recorded *Please Please Me*, the song that was to give them their first No. 1 hit on 16 February 1963, and I had gone back to *NME*. In their collarless jackets the Beatles joined the Mini motorcar, the mini-skirt and Ian Fleming's hero James Bond 007 as the symbols of a new Britain. An explosion of success ensued culminating in that magic April night on which (according to the following day's papers) Beatlemania was born.

The four had quickly got used to fans screaming during their performances but it was what happened as they made their exit from the Royal Albert Hall after performing *Please Please*

Me, From Me To You and *Twist and Shout* to an ecstatic reception during a pop concert staged by the BBC. Up to that point no one had ever seen a mobbing like it. While a crowd of fans blocked the road preventing the Austin Princess limousine hired to take them back to the Royal Court Hotel in Sloane Square, several climbed on to the roof of the car. The noise was frightening and I should know, I'd squeezed in alongside them and regretted it almost immediately.

Eventually the police managed to clear a path for their getaway, but not before several helmets had been sent flying. The problem was, where to go now. The Ad Lib Club off Leicester Square was their usual nightly haunt but a very nervous George pointed out that there would already be hundreds of people making their way there.

'You can come back to my flat,' I volunteered, rather rashly. Strictly speaking, it was not my flat at all. I rented a bedsitter in a rather nice Chelsea apartment at the top of King's House in King's Road. My live-in landlords were a veteran actress called Dorothy Dickson and her husband who was the international buyer for the upmarket London store, Liberty. As luck would have it they were away on holiday so I had the place to myself that night. On the way I picked up a couple of bottles of Mateus rosé.

'Just two bottles?' said John. 'Afraid so,' I replied. I hadn't planned on entertaining so many guests since the number swelled by three with the arrival of the singer Shane Fenton (later known as Alvin Stardust and now sadly deceased), his girlfriend Susan, and the actress Jane Asher who had been at the Albert Hall to interview the Beatles for Radio Times. All had to climb three flights of stone stairs to get to the third floor flat.

There were not enough chairs in the front room so the Regency furniture was pushed back and we all sat on the green-carpeted floor. Initially the conversation was about the near-riot, which had taken place outside the Albert Hall barely an hour earlier.

'I nearly had me bleedin' head ripped off,' said Ringo sipping his drink. 'If it goes on like this someone's goin' to get seriously hurt.'

'Yeah, or seriously rich,' said John, never one to miss a chance.

I raised my precious glass of the Mateus, then the sophisticated drink for the young in this posh part of London. None of us knew anything about vintages or high living, but we were willing to learn.

'To the Beatles.'

John narrowed his eyes and spoke in that superior Scouse drawl. 'Yeah, the group the fans love so much they want to tear us to pieces.'

Miss Asher, the sophisticated one in the group, laughed. 'Oh John, you're such a cynic. Admit it . . . you adore the attention.'

He tasted his drink and licked his lips. 'Sure, I'm a cynic. What we play is just rock'n'roll under a new name. Rock music is war – hostility and conquest. We sing about love, but we mean sex – and *they* know it.'

'*They* think you're decent, clean-living blokes,' I said.

'It's just an image,' said John, 'and the one we've got is wrong. Look at the Rolling Stones. Rough as guts. We did that first and now they've pinched it thanks to Brian [Epstein] and his suits.'

'You can't blame Eppy for that,' said Ringo introducing a note of reason.

'The fans have to dream that one day they might marry a Beatle,' said Jane.

'Yeah, but only the girls who have yet to reach the age of puberty,' said John. 'I give some girl an autograph and she wants my tie or a handful of my hair. Then she wants to have *me*. Then she tells me she's only 15. Jailbait. Is there any more booze?'

I poured the last of the wine from the flask-shaped bottle into John's glass. 'That's the last of it. I'll see if Dorothy has any more lying about.'

In a kitchen cupboard I found half a bottle of Gordon's Gin which was surprising since, judging by the dark glasses Mrs Dickson always wore when we passed outside the shared bathroom in the morning, I doubted she ever left any drink lying around.

John downed most before going to search though the bedside cupboard in my tiny room. He returned clutching a small bottle of amphetamines, which my mother had sent me from our home in Torquay. Her doctor prescribed them for slimming.

'Ah Crispy,' said the-Beatle-that-bit. 'Shades of Hamburg, eh?'

Tongues were loosened once the pills had taken effect. That was not good news for Miss Asher. John bombarded her with some offensively intimate questions. I intervened in a manner, which did not please him.

'Oh fab. No booze and now insults from the host. What kind of night is this?'

No one was up to reminding him that this was the night the Beatles had become the most exciting music act Britain had ever known. All eyes were on the girl with a mane of red hair that cascaded down below her shoulders: Jane was quietly weeping.

It was a perfect party-killing moment. Aware that he was no longer in danger of being discovered by a marauding mob, John got up from the floor while George comforted Jane. But it was Paul who escorted the teenager with the cut-glass accent back down the stone steps and into the night. Whatever words passed between them as they strolled along

King's Road in search of a taxi, they clearly worked, for Paul and Jane subsequently became engaged and were together for the next five years.

Jane Asher went on to marry the cartoonist Gerald Scarfe in 1981. McCartney said he was sorry to have lost her.

4

NEW YORK

ONE of those who read about the outbreak of Beatlemania in Britain was Sidney Bernstein, a hard-nosed, down-on-his-luck, New York-based promoter. Having pored over newspaper items about what was happening to the musical phenomenon on the other side of the Atlantic, it became an obsession with Sid to stage them in concert in the US long before he had even heard, let alone seen, them.

From 'a friend of a friend' he managed to get hold of Brian Epstein's private number and from his shoebox of an office in the Bronx he called the manager in London. According to Sid, the conversation went like this: 'Mr Epstein, my name is Sid Bernstein. I am a promoter here in New York and I would like to present your group in America. I have been reading about them for months, never heard a song. There are no records being played here and nobody in America seems to care about British music, but I would like to play the Beatles.'

Now Epstein was well aware that at that point America was a no-no for the group. Capitol Records, the US arm of EMI, did not want to put out their records because the company did not think they would sell in an American market. So the rights to records that were selling in tens of thousands across Europe, were passed in America to smaller labels. Obsessed Sid, however, persisted and asked Epstein how much he would charge for the Beatles to give a concert in the US. The charming but naive manager had no idea how much to ask. He mentioned they had just been paid $2,000 for a single show in the UK. Bernstein said he would pay them $6,500 for two shows at New York's Carnegie Hall (he didn't mention that he would have to borrow the money both for the fee and the deposit required to reserve the venue).

Epstein was overwhelmed. So much money and the one and only Carnegie Hall. They agreed a date: it was to be Wednesday 12 February 1964. That was Lincoln's birthday, Bernstein was keen to point out. Still faced with Capitol's reluctance to back the Beatles, Epstein flew to New York to try and stir things up. He took with him their recording of *I Want to Hold Your Hand*, a song John and Paul had written at Jane Asher's London home in Wimpole Street.

At about the same time as Epstein was US-bound, America's No. 1 TV host Ed Sullivan was passing through London Airport (renamed Heathrow two years later) with his wife. He witnessed a scene that aroused his interest: hundreds of teenagers holding aloft 'LONG LIVE THE BEATLES' and 'THE BEATLES FOR EVER' banners were waiting to welcome John, Paul, George and Ringo home from Stockholm where they had been performing on Swedish television.

Never the hippest of men despite the colossal success of his peak-time Sunday night *Ed Sullivan Show* on network television, the presenter was curious. The Beatles? The newspaper columnist-turned-TV host thought it must be a circus act and went in search of further information. Ever mindful of the fact that he had once turned down the act that later went on to give him his highest viewing figure to date – Elvis – Sullivan did some homework. He learned that Sid Bernstein had already booked them to appear at Carnegie Hall the following February.

Back in New York, Sullivan and Bernstein met to compare notes. Pushed along by the promoter's enthusiasm for an act he also hadn't seen, the TV host sought out the visiting Brian

Epstein and booked the Beatles to appear on his show – normally dominated by crooners, comedians and acrobats – on 9 February – three days before their New York concert date.

Meanwhile, an American disc jockey got an advance copy of *I Want to Hold Your Hand* from his girlfriend, a BOAC stewardess. He played it and was besieged by callers begging him to play it again. So he did and by that sheer fluke Capitol rushed the disc out and put a promotional budget of $40,000 behind the bar. Word of the record spread like wildfire and within days it had gone to No. 1.

Now here's the secret: it wasn't until they topped the US charts that Brian Epstein told the Beatles about the deal he had made with Sullivan. The celebration party at their suite in the George V in Paris during their Olympia engagement was so raucous, that Epstein danced with the men he called his 'boys', wearing a chamber pot on his head.

The chaps from Liverpool who I had met backstage at a grotty club in Hamburg, were about to become four of the most famous people on the planet.

* * *

THE Beatles arrived in New York on Friday 7 February. To their astonishment, there were thousands of fans waiting when their Pan Am flight touched down. It has to be said here that the welcome owed much to the offer of a dollar and a free Beatles T-shirt broadcast by two local radio stations which had been talked into the hype by a sharp operator who had bought merchandising rights to the group from a very naive Brian Epstein. Thousands of 'The Beatles Are Coming' bumper stickers bought from the Capitol Records promotion budget also helped.

I joined them at the Plaza Hotel. All four wanted to go out and take their first glimpse of an American city, but the NYPD forbade it. By now New York was gripped with Beatle fever: they were front-page headlines in the newspapers and the main topic of conversation on both TV and radio news.

There was something of a carnival atmosphere at the CBS studio when they turned up for the first of what was now a three-show booking to appear on Sullivan's programme. The radio in their dressing room was playing Beatles records non-stop. 'It's like Liddypool [Liverpool] on a Saturday night,' joked Ringo. If the joke sounded forced then no wonder.

This was to be the biggest night of the Fab Four's collective life. The appearance was bound to make them stars in America.

As Neil Aspinall, their road manager, laid out the new outfits Epstein had ordered specially from their London tailor, John let out a groan: 'This shirt needs cuff links. I've got no bloody cuff links.'

'I have,' I said, swiftly removing the imitation gold fasteners from my own cuffs. 'You can borrow them but I want them back – they were a present.

A present in fact from Don Arden, the rogue promoter who had inadvertently brought us together by sending me to Hamburg to take care of Little Richard.

John took the cheap jewellery and examined it before placing the links in his own cuffs, noticing that the motifs adorning them were two theatrical masks, one a happy face, the other sad. 'Just like me,' he said. 'Very appropriate Crispy.'

I walked down two flights of stairs with them to the studios and seconds later they were on with an estimated 73 million Americans – about 40 per cent of the population – watching. They sang *All My Loving, Till There Was You* and *She Loves You* as Ed Sullivan stood in the wings, open-mouthed at the reaction they were getting from the studio audience. Before the show ended they returned to perform *I Saw Her Standing There* and their No. 1 hit *I Want to Hold Your Hand*. Their future was assured. Nothing could stand in their way now. Nothing.

Later, from the window of their suite on the 12th floor of the Plaza, John and Paul surveyed the scene below. Barriers manned by scores of police had been erected to keep at bay thousands of fans who were to maintain an all-night vigil singing: 'We love you Beatles, oh yes we do' between bursts of screaming.

'I guess the same thing happens every time Elvis hits town,' said Paul overawed by the sight before him.

'Elvis?' said John somewhat dismissively, 'Oh aye, Elvis Pretzel,' adding, 'He's never even played New York', conveniently forgetting that the Beatles own debut concert was still some days away.

It seemed a convenient moment to remind John about the promise he had extracted from me back in Hamburg, to try and arrange a meeting for him with the King of Rock'n'Roll.

'I'll phone Colonel Parker and see if I can set something up,' I said moving to a telephone positioned on a nearby writing bureau.

Since he was now a regular phone pal, I had no difficulty getting through to the Colonel on the other side of the country. All four Beatles listened in as Parker – who had sent them a telegram on Elvis's behalf – began the conversation with, as usual, a pitch about money. He wanted to know how much Epstein had got the Beatles for their Sullivan Show appearance. '$10,000,' I was able to tell him. 'I knew that,' he replied. 'I was just checking to see if you knew. He should have got me to negotiate the deal. I got $50,000 for Elvis and that was back in '56.'

I did my best to sound impressed, hoping that would give me some leverage in the favour I was angling for.

'Colonel, I'm sure you've thought of it already, but what about fixing a meeting between Elvis and the Beatles?'

He considered the question for a few moments.

'You know these guys pretty well, huh?'

'Sure. If you watched the TV closely you might have noticed the cuff links John Lennon was wearing. They're mine.'

'A meeting, huh? It did cross my mind. Sure, why not? Tell 'em they can visit us any time they like.'

'Er, they sort of thought Elvis might visit them.'

In response, Parker became business-like, quite gruff: 'Let me tell you something, son. Elvis Presley is an international entertainer – perhaps the most famous in the world - a Hollywood movie star. A couple of weeks ago I told him I hoped American teenagers would be as good to the Beatles as they had been to us. Elvis said he felt the same way. He's on holiday in Las Vegas at the moment but I'll pass on your suggestion to him.'

And so the business of a meeting between the American megastar and his four new British rivals would have to wait. Having been glued to their TV sets for the previous 48 hours, Presley and Parker were both acutely aware that a meteor with the Beatles name on it had just struck the US and neither of the Americans was in abdication mode.

The phone call concluded, John – ever a capricious character – made it clear he had picked up on Parker's nuances. 'Next time you speak to the Colonel,' he said, 'tell him Elvis can visit us any time – just like his fans are doing.'

The following day, the Beatles awoke to a New York covered in snow, but nothing short of a blizzard would have driven away the army of fans camped outside. For the group, it was to be business as usual: they were to give a press conference. Facing a bemused corps of reporters, photographers and TV cameramen, they answered some pretty silly questions from serious men and women who clearly thought they should be doing something more important. Invited to enter battle with the *New York Times* over a scathing review their *Ed Sullivan Show* debut had received, John delivered a typical Lennon response: 'It's all lies.' At that stage, however, no one understood his humour.

It was interesting to note that afterwards their cynical interrogators asked the Beatles for their autographs, prefacing their requests with remarks like 'It's not for me, you understand. It's for my kids.'

From New York the Beatles circus, as it had become, travelled south to Washington D.C. where the group were to give their first live US concert at the Coliseum/Sports Arena. I watched from the back with Brian Epstein. A cop standing alongside us stuck a bullet in each ear to shut out the shattering sound of thousands of girls screaming. The scene made the cover of the next issue of Newsweek. When jelly beans, much harder than the jelly babies the fans threw in Britain, rained down on the stage, Paul was obliged to appeal: 'Please throw peppermint creams, they're softer when they hit us.'

Later I witnessed another example of John's refusal to suffer fools gladly when the Beatles (somewhat reluctantly, Epstein admitted) agreed to be guests of honour at a masked ball put on by the British ambassador Sir David Ormsby-Gore at the British Embassy.

Already angered by the sight of a woman using a pair of nail scissors to hack off a lock of Ringo's hair, John had refused to sign his name for a young British aristoprat who had shoved an autograph book in his face. 'You will sign it and like it,' the toff persisted. 'Oh really,' replied John before turning on his heels to walk out on a shocked ambassador and his grand guests.

'They're treating us like animals,' he said back at the hotel. Just like the animals Sullivan thought they must be that day he saw the Beatle banners at London Airport.

The following day they took the train back to New York where they made Sid Bernstein the happiest man in the U.S. by selling all 6,000 tickets for their two concerts at Carnegie Hall – just as he and Epstein had agreed when the Beatles were relatively unknown in the U.S. – on Lincoln's birthday. It was an astonishing success. Backstage the promoter wept: 'I could have sold 200,000 tickets,' he wailed. 'Why didn't I book them for the whole week?'

Then it was off to Miami, Florida for the second of their TV dates with Ed Sullivan. John, who had stayed in a rage following the embassy incident in Washington, finally unwound when the group were taken on a pleasure cruise on the yacht *Southern Trail*, courtesy of a friendly millionaire.

'Funny 'ow these people all have swimming pools when the sea is just at the bottom of their gardens,' said Ringo as the craft skirted white-walled mansions lining the waterside.

'Well, this isn't Merseyside – they wear mink bikinis here,' quipped John.

As the yacht passed a small beach, someone recognised the 'Mopheads', as the Beatles had become known across

America and dozens of hands waved in greeting. 'So it's not just in New York that we're famous,' deadpanned George.

Back at the Deauville Hotel from where the next Sullivan show was to be televised, they were treated to a lobster and champagne bash. George asked me if I remembered them cadging steaks from Little Richard in Hamburg little more than a year earlier. 'No more of that now we've cracked the US,' he said, 'From now on it's Kentucky Fried Chicken!' The following day he was taken sick with food poisoning. He sent me a message: 'That's the last time I let you order the food!'

Over on the West Coast, Elvis wasn't allowing himself to be completely upstaged by the visitors. He posed obligingly on his yacht *Potomac* for a picture that would be used on a two-page magazine spread about the Beatles. 'I wish they were here in person,' he said sounding somewhat disingenuous. 'They're not competition; they're an asset to the music business – keeping it fresh and alive.'

Obviously not having a clue about the distance involved, John, Paul, George and Ringo became excited when they were told that Elvis was sailing *Potomac* to Florida to meet them. The story was a hoax. Elvis's yacht stayed in the coastal waters off California. The summit meeting would just have to wait.

***

AS an introduction to America, the short stay had proved a success beyond Brian Epstein's wildest dreams. They deserved every cheer they got when the plane bringing them home landed at Heathrow. It had become apparent even to their worst enemies that the Beatles were no seven-day wonders.

In April they made a TV special for Rediffusion called *Around the Beatles*, which included, as well as a selection of their fast-growing hits, a sketch from *A Midsummer Night's Dream*. John appeared as Thisbe, Paul as Pyramus, George as Moonshine and Ringo as the Lion, each of them reluctantly wearing Shakespearean costumes.

No sooner was that done than it was time to start work on their first film: about 24 hours in the life of the group. John had wanted to call the film 'Authenticity' and Roy Orbison, who I took to the set at Twickenham Studios, suggested 'Ben Hair', but in the end director Dick Lester settled for Ringo's suggestion, *A Hard Day's Night*, a phrase he had contributed to John's first book, *In His Own Write*. Orbison was not displeased to learn that his suggestion had not been taken up: when he arrived at the studios John was filming a scene in a bath. 'Hey Orbison, bet you don't get to take six baths a day.' 'No,' the droll American replied, 'but I don't need 'em.' The friendly banter had defused the situation when Roy was obliged to hand over his headline billing to the Beatles when they toured the UK together. Even a big international star like him could not follow the screaming adulation John, Paul, George and Ringo received every time they appeared on stage.

By now the pressure on the tour was enormous and it was inevitable that sooner or later one of them would crack. It was Ringo. He collapsed during a picture session just a couple of days before the Beatles were due to leave for a tour of Scandinavia, the Far East and Australia. I was with them when it happened and noticed the shock on the faces of the others as their drummer sank to his knees. Rather in the manner of Frank Sinatra poking fun at Sammy Davis Jnr when the Rat Pack were on stage, Ringo had frequently been the butt of John's jibes. Once, when they were asked if

Ringo was the best drummer in the world, John quipped, 'He's not even the best drummer in the Beatles.'

Now nobody was laughing. Ringo was rushed to hospital. The tour dates ahead could not be cancelled so a drummer called Jimmy Nicol was brought in as his temporary replacement.

Happily Ringo was able to re-join the group in Melbourne and they never played without him again.

Soon after they got back to the UK the group found themselves in Liverpool for the northern premiere of *A Hard Day's Night*. At the civic reception, which followed, there was a virtual re-run of the Washington embassy incident. A local dignitary grabbed John's arm just as he was picking up a sandwich.

'Careful, that's my bad arm,' said the Beatle sounding a note of warning. 'Sign this,' snapped the notable paying no heed to his quip. John took the book and pen with one hand and thrust the sandwich into the man's mouth saying 'Hold this.' After writing in the book (I never did find out what he wrote) he handed it back to the astonished owner and crossed the room to join the others, leaving the shocked and now not-so-dignified dignitary with the sandwich clenched between his teeth.

It was becoming apparent that the Beatles were being forcibly accepted in a world that did not understand them and they were fast developing a way of coping with people who assumed they hailed from a sub-normal species. I began scribbling down items of Beatle-speak, quotes which came in response to inane questions, like when Ringo was asked how he liked girls to dress: 'In dresses', he responded. When someone asked George what he thought of topless swimsuits he quipped, 'Fine, I've been wearing them for years.' And when an inquisitor of John demanded to know why the Beatles' music excited people so much, he delivered this explanation, 'If we knew we'd form another group and become managers.'

For many, The Beatles appearance on The Ed Sullivan Show was a defining moment comparable to "Where were you when Kennedy was shot?" or man's first steps on the moon. After their final appearance on the show, however, Sullivan was to admit that before he committed to signing them he called America's No. 1 news presenter, Walter Cronkite, to ask him what he knew about 'those bugs, or whatever they call themselves.' His inability to remember the group's name was typical Sullivan.

5

WEYBRIDGE

I NEVER was quite sure why John wanted to see me when, one Saturday morning, he summoned me to Kenwood, the home he had just paid £18,000* for on the ultra-exclusive St George's Hill estate in Weybridge. The location was a surprise for a start, for this was the Surrey stockbroker belt. His neighbours were among the richest, most elite members of the establishment for whom he had expressed nothing but contempt in our past discussions about life. (He was surprised that they laughed when he urged those in the most expensive seats to 'rattle your jewellery' during the Beatles Royal Variety Show appearance. It was an admonishment and he had intended it as an insult).

Built half a century earlier, Kenwood was a massive mock-Tudor mansion with 22 rooms and an acre-and-a-half of garden. It was very un-Beatle, but then so was the man who greeted me at the front door. John was wearing a green corduroy suit, over a bright red sweater – not at all the uniform of a rock star. 'What do you think of the clobber then? I've got a flat cap to match. It's what people around here seem to wear and I suppose I ought to make an effort to fit in,' he said noting the look of surprise on my face. Oh dear, I thought. My friend has escaped from one goldfish bowl only to land in another.

The next surprise was his apparent fascination with the domestic arrangements of his new property acquisition. He began by showing off the split-level kitchen. It was very St George's Hill, very non-John Lennon. Cynthia (the 'secret' wife he'd whispered existence of back in the Hamburg days) proudly demonstrated how to handle 'the gadgets', but admitted, 'I had to get someone down from London to show me how the knobs and switches worked.' 'I'm like you,' said John, 'I'm used to the stove up against the wall.' The cooker was set on an island in the centre of the room under a giant extractor hood and would have made a splendid feature for *Ideal Home*. Definitely not *Rolling Stone*.

No, this was definitely not rock'n'roll and I was surprised – shocked even – to find a rebel like John Lennon seeming to take such an interest in home-making. In reality, I suspect he was at least as uncomfortable as me in the surroundings, but he was doing his best to like it for Cynthia's sake. Clearly nervous, Mrs John Lennon rustled up a meal of bacon, egg and chips and served it to us seated on the kitchen stools. It didn't seem right.

The grand tour followed: the largest of the six reception rooms had black carpets, two huge sofas and a marble fireplace. On the other side of it was the dining room, hideously decorated with purple velvet wallpaper.

The bedrooms – five on the first floor, one on the floor above – were substantial, all with ensuite bathrooms, and the master bedroom had a huge sunken bath. There were John Lewis-style paintings everywhere, but hung in one of the guest bedrooms were just two drawings and our host became clearly emotional when he explained they were there for 'sentimental reasons'. They were in fact works by his late dear friend, the man who helped him found the Beatles, Stuart Sutcliffe.

In that moment all John's feelings for the one man he had most liked and admired became apparent, he turned away but not before I saw his eyes welled up with tears. John never liked looking back when it exposed his feelings – indeed he had told Stuart's girlfriend Astrid Kirchherr to face up to the situation - 'either die with him or go on living' - when they discussed the unexpected death of the man they both loved. But even he could do nothing to hide the sadness brought on by such reminders of the past as hung before us.

We left the 'Sutcliffe room' and I noticed that he locked the door behind him. The room had become a shrine.

Recovering his composure he led me back on to the landing, pausing briefly at a window to survey the garden: 'I'm going to have a swimming pool out there,' he said. But paddling in a pool was clearly not what he had on his mind.

Downstairs, on the yellow sofa where he was to spend most of his time, he came to the point of our meeting: 'Guess who's surfaced? Who's floated to the top of the scum? Me flamin' dad, that's who. He turned up here the other day on the bloody doorstep and Cyn let him in – she even fed him cheese on toast and gave him a haircut while they waited for me to get back from wherever. Thankfully he'd left by the time I got home.'

Born in Liverpool in December 1912, one of eight children living in a single room, Freddie Lennon had first set eyes on John's mother Julia when she was just 15. After an eleven-year courtship they married in 1938 and Julia was already pregnant with John when Lennon senior was sent to sea working on merchant convoys. Father and son spent some time together when John was just 18 months old but this was wartime and they were soon separated again. When Freddie returned in 1944, Julia was pregnant again – with another man's child. The marriage was just about over.

'He turned up a few weeks ago at Eppy's office in London,' he said after a few moments of reflective pause. 'In a bit of a panic, Brian had let him into the inner sanctum after he'd told the receptionist he was my father. I was actually there and watched him in Eppy's room through a little window. He had somebody with him and I figured they were on the make so I went into the office and asked them in no uncertain manner to leave. Why would he surface after all this time if it wasn't because of what I'd become?

'Apparently he's been cleaning dishes in the kitchens at a pub not far from here. A coincidence? I don't think so. I just wish he'd get on with whatever life he had and let me get on with mine. Too much water under the bridge.'

So that was it. John wanted to talk. His mind was troubled by his father's experience and he had no neighbour on this affluent estate he could confide in about matters of dysfunctional family strife in the working class area of a distant northern city.

Freddie Lennon was the immediate problem; the late Julia Lennon was the underlying one. 'I lost my Mum twice,' he suddenly proclaimed from his throne – the yellow sofa. 'Once, when I was five and she put me with me auntie (Julia's sister, Mimi Smith) and then again when she died [as she crossed the road outside Mimi's home to catch a bus home].' Julia was knocked down by a car driven by an off-duty policeman and died instantly on the evening of 15 July 1958.

Although his mother had forsaken him to pursue a hedonistic path, John was shattered by her sudden death. But not for long. He had come to admire the fact that she had chosen a life of freedom rather than one of responsibility and once he was over the immediate grief he revelled in the notion that now he had responsibilities to no one. Mimi put food on the table and clothes on his back, but Julia, eccentric

Julia, had always been the interesting one. She would walk out in public wearing a pair of old-fashioned knickers on her head with the legs hanging down over her back. I have often wondered if such behaviour inspired John some years later when he sat on the front row of the Troubador in Los Angeles for a performance by the Smothers Brothers with a tampon fastened to his forehead.

What could I say that might help? Little, except that we are powerless over other people, places and things as I had learned from the bitter experience of my own father's passing which had wrecked our family.

It did not stop John from rambling on as afternoon turned into evening and our wives talked practical matters in another room. I got his message - his cynicism owed much to the troubled relationship of his parents. His disrespect for authority, however, owed much to the fact that the policeman's colleagues did not arrest him for causing the death of his mother although John was told there were clear indications that the driver was drunk. Julia was 44, John, back then, was 17.

The sheer luxury of his comfortable, if ostentatious, surroundings did nothing to relieve the pain of the past. 'It's all right for you,' he said at one point, 'you can go out walking with your wife and live a regular life. I bloody can't. We live in a sort of prison now and it looks as though it's going to be that way for ever.'

That evening I drove the four of us into London to wine the night away (still Mateus rosé!) at the Ad Lib. The Ad Lib was a disco atop the Prince Charles Cinema off Leicester Square. This was the hip place for the movers and groovers of what *Time* magazine was calling 'Swinging London'. John loved being at the Ad Lib because he needed to feel part of something other than the Beatles. He had to be with his own kind – the artists, musicians, beauticians, hairdressers and other young people of the night – not the aspiring business types of stock-broking Surrey.

We slipped into one of the banquettes and ordered Mateus rosé, still the recommended drink for young trendies, and looked at each other in the glow of the red glass candleholders on each table. John and Cyn were both extremely short-sighted, but refused to be seen wearing glasses in public. As they hadn't got around to trying the new contact lenses yet, they had no alternative but to blink myopically at the passing parade. Girls danced in Quant skirts, providing the only floorshow. Regular as clockwork, Ringo, the relentless clubman, turned up, and Brian put in an appearance before disappearing on one of his furtive sorties.

However, the showstopper was Alma Cogan, the 'girl with the giggle in her voice'. Even in the semi-darkness, her theatrical make-up glowed brightly. Everybody loved Alma, but John was totally smitten. She was the secret love of his life. He told me that she reminded him in some respects – in temperament if not appearance – of his mother, who had loved being the life and soul of the party. Both had a mischievous sense of humour and both loved singing, dancing and flirting. 'Every time I'm with Alma, it feels right,' said John. 'Julia just couldn't cope with me, but Alma can read me like a book.'

In the Fifties, Alma had risen to be Britain's highest-paid female singer, her strapless ball gowns becoming as famous as the cute songs she sang, such as *Never Do a Tango with an Eskimo, Where Will the Baby's Dimple Be?* and *He Couldn't Resist Her Pocket Transistor* – the last one even made her a household name in Japan.

For John, it had been love at first sight the moment that he met Alma during a party at the Knightsbridge home of

Maurice Kinn, then the owner of the *NME* and my boss. In the weeks that followed, John and the other Beatles had been regular attenders at Alma's parties held in her flat at 44 Stafford Court on Kensington High Street, along with Cary Grant, Noël Coward, Stanley Baker and Lionel Bart. Whenever anyone asked why she had never married, Alma's message was: 'Some people go to a psychiatrist, others get married. In any case, I buy my own minks.'

Cyn never wanted to compete for John in such glamorous company. She dressed poorly, being by nature neither ambitious nor free spending enough to be daring even though John was by then a millionaire. (I don't believe she thought that the money would last.) This night, as Len Barry's ubiquitous *1-2-3* boomed over the speakers and Alma sparkled for her boyfriend, the Ad Lib's manager Brian Morris, Cyn made suburban remarks and John became annoyed. After the freedom of the bedroom that he had come to take for granted on tour, it was obvious that Cyn was not the one he wanted at his side. There was a frosty silence in the back of the Jag as I drove the Lennons home to Weybridge.

At this stage of his life, John was searching for a woman who could be both lover and mother, a dual role that Cyn could never hope to fulfil. But it was apparent that he was more infatuated with Alma than she was with him, although this never prevented him from trying to win her over. She was accustomed to the attentions of lovesick young men, and John was just one of many who tried to gain her favours.

In retrospect, the similarities between John and Elvis are marked, right down to the search for surrogate mother love, the escapist drug taking, the spiritual quest and even their problems with food. John had a tendency towards obesity because of his indiscriminate drinking, drugging and eating. When someone referred to him as the 'Fat Beatle', he became obsessed with his weight.

'Every tour we go on, John decides to slim – and, believe me, this involves quite a performance,' the Beatles road manager (and later president of their Apple empire) Neil Aspinall told me at the time. 'John's natural weight is 159 pounds but he's got a bit of a spare tyre round his middle and he does everything to try to lose it. He sticks to one main meal a day: steak and salad, no vegetables.

'What John can't see is how Paul weighs roughly the same as him and yet looks so slim. It's just that they are built differently, of course. John has two sets of suits – one for when he is his normal weight and the other for when he has slimmed down to a trimmer figure.'

As the DJ played *1-2-3* yet again, John turned to face me in the dim glow of the table top candles which burned in small scarlet glasses, and said: 'Tell me again, how did your dad die?'

'He killed himself,' I replied.

'Wish mine would,' he responded.

Suffering a pang of conscience, John subsequently made friends with his father and invited him to move in to Kenwood with his young bride, Pauline Jones, who busied herself answering fan mail which arrived from around the world by the sack load. Alas, the relationship did not last and John subsequently bought the couple a home of their own in Brighton.

Alma Cogan died on 21 October 1966. She was just 34

*Kenwood was last sold for almost £14 million.

6

USA COAST-TO-COAST

NOW the hottest act on earth, the Beatles arrived in San Francisco for their first coast-to-coast tour of the US in August, 1964. I was with them.

During the transatlantic flight, Paul, George and Ringo all seemed in high spirits with George at one point dancing in the aisle to music he was listening to on his headphones. Positioned in the seat next to mine for the 13-hour journey, John launched into a depressing conversation about how he had become a great worrier: 'I'm terrified to even lift a phone and book a table in a restaurant,' he confided. The real cause of his anxiety was fear. He said he had a premonition that he would die in tragic circumstances. He was, he admitted, over another scotch and coke, 'paranoid about somebody trying to bump me off'.

I knew he was serious, having seen him soaked in sweat before a concert, terrified at the thought of facing 'the mob' as he sometimes referred to the audience. Scanning the itinerary of the tour ahead, he stopped at one name and said: 'Dallas – that's where Lee Harvey Oswald shot Kennedy. That reminds me, I've got something to show you.'

And with that he produced a crumpled piece of typewritten paper and read from it: 'Kennedy was assassinated on a Friday – so was Lincoln. They were both shot from behind, in the head on a Friday and in the presence of their wives. Lincoln was elected in 1860, Kennedy in 1960. Both of their successors were named Johnson and were southern democrats. Lincoln's killer shot him in a theatre and ran to a warehouse. Oswald shot Kennedy from a warehouse and ran to a theatre.

'So what?' I said, trying to lighten the mood. 'So it's uncanny,' said John folding the paper before handing it to me. 'These psychopaths must follow some sort of pattern. I wonder if Kennedy ever worried that it might happen to him [the president had been assassinated in Dallas just nine months earlier].'

Oh dear, this was no mood to be in at the start of what was promised to be an incredibly successful tour, since every seat had been sold out well in advance. Seated in the row behind us, Epstein was clearly nervous too. He had asked the promoters to ensure that the limousines sent to meet them at San Francisco airport were closed cars instead of the open models originally planned. George had jokingly said, 'And we'd like bullet-proof vests.'

Although happy on this flight, George was the Beatle most troubled by the way things with the fans were changing: 'Previously pop stars have been put on a pedestal – unreachable. But our image has always been a different one. We were the ones you could come up to, shake hands with and say "You're doing a great job, whacker." We liked it that way, but now it's just impossible.'

In San Francisco the Beatles got their taste of what the local police chief described as 'presidential treatment'. For the first concert of their twenty-four city tour they were collected by a limousine which actually wound its way up a drive inside the hotel. Once they were safely aboard the limos were then driven the wrong way down one-way roads to the Cow Palace stadium with an escort of police motorcyclists, their sirens wailing and blue and red lights flashing, to make sure that nothing got in the way.

Waiting to greet them backstage were a host of celebrities including the actress Shirley Temple and the singer Joan Baez. Waiting out front were 17,000 fans who were preparing to scream their way through a 45-minute performance of ten Beatle songs.

Once the concert was over they were to be rushed back to the waiting limos, outriders already in position, to be whisked back to the airport they had arrived at such a short time earlier. At least that was the plan since the police had made it a condition that they left town as soon as their work was done. Alas, things didn't work out that way: a decoy police car sped off from the backstage area but no one was being fooled. The limousine carrying the four was quickly spotted and – just as had happened outside the Royal Albert Hall at the start of Beatlemania the previous year – many had jumped on the roof making it unsafe. Officers seconded an ambulance which had been taking several intoxicated sailors to hospital, unloaded its drunken cargo and pushed the Beatles inside.

Once they arrived at the airport, it was another run to the waiting chartered airliner which had been chartered to transport them around America for the 25-city tour.

And so the somewhat disheveled party flew into Las Vegas's McCarran Airport at 2am that night, with both manager and all four musicians in a worried state. Events in San Francisco had proved that they had reason to be concerned; security had to be stepped up. There would, however, always be a gap in the fence somewhere and this was evidenced by the arrival of a female fan at the door of their suite at the Sands Hotel the following afternoon. Somehow she had got through a cordon of guards in the lobby and two – one at the lift and the other at the suite door itself – to find herself in the lounge overlooking The Strip where I was sharing a drink with the somewhat jaded Beatles.

How she had achieved this was revealed in her cheery introduction: 'Hi guys, I'm Donald O'Connor's daughter.'

Her father was a Hollywood legend so even the guards had been unable to bar her.

John was not impressed: 'Oh, I'm sorry love, I really am.'

The star's puzzled daughter asked, 'Whaddya mean, you're sorry?'

In a statement he would later so bitterly regret, he said: 'Just heard it on the radio about your dad. You must be grief stricken.'

The atmosphere in the room froze. Everyone stared at John but no one could find words to utter. Mr O'Connor's daughter broke down in hysterics, help was summoned and she was sedated before being taken away by paramedics. It was left to someone else to give her the good news that her Hollywood legend father was, in fact, alive and in the best of health.

John could be cruel at times and I know that his sharp cutting edge was a protection against his own insecurity, that he could be his own worst enemy. But this time he had gone too far. A few hours passed before I dared raise mention of the incident. 'Soft cow,' he said. 'Why the hell did she think we'd care about who her father was. It's always "I'm the mayor's wife" or "My brother knows the president". Well *I'm* a Beatle but I don't go around boasting about it.'"

By now one of the four best-known men on the planet, John, of course, had no need to state the obvious to anyone he met. However, his inability to grasp the difference between himself and a nervous, excited fan was a clear indication that he was in danger of losing the plot. The strain of being a Beatle was starting to show and it was a clear and present signal of danger ahead.

'John never gets openly angry, but when someone annoys him – and fools always do – he can tear them to shreds with his sarcasm,' Neil Aspinall said. 'It's impossible to win a verbal battle with John. I've seen many famous, important people learn that lesson the hard way.'

John was also scornful of the way people imitated Beatle fashions. He could not conceal his contempt when a TV news bulletin reported that showbiz stars including Steve McQueen were flocking to a Hollywood barber who was specialising in Beatle haircuts. 'And McQueen was one of my heroes. How soft can you get?' he snorted.

He was equally disdainful when it was reported that those without sufficient hair of their own – among them, the world's richest man at that time, J. Paul Getty – were wearing Beatle wigs. 'The only rich guy I'm interested in is Howard Hughes,' John said. 'I bet he doesn't wear a Beatle wig.'

John was hugely intrigued by Hughes, who was living at the Desert Inn just a short distance from the Sands. Hughes had arrived in Las Vegas one midnight the previous year, travelling incognito in the back of an ambulance – just as the Beatles had left San Francisco. Guarded by his Mormon entourage, he had entered the hotel through the back door and occupied all the high-roller suites on the ninth floor. There he had stayed, seeing no one except his immediate staff. Not even the armed Mormons stationed at the entrances to his suite had set eyes on him.

Hughes's reclusive lifestyle so fascinated John that he took a big risk with his own safety. While thousands of fans were camped outside the Sands hoping to catch a glimpse of the Fab Four, it was John's wish to see the reclusive billionaire's hiding place for himself. When he put his request to the security guards, they told him it was impossible and refused to take responsibility for any Beatle venturing beyond the heavily guarded suite which had become their prison cell. But John was so determined to visit the Desert Inn that he recruited the help of Irving Kandell, the concert programme concessionaire who was also a staunch Beatle fan and who had already said he would do anything he could to make their stay enjoyable as well as profitable.

Kandell, the son of a Greek immigrant, who always introduced himself as 'Oiving – that's Irving with an O', was as good as his word. He borrowed a hotel doorman's uniform and a catering van, and enlisted my help to smuggle John down a flight of back stairs, through the kitchens and into the forbidden world beyond. No one recognized the Beatle, disguised in the doorman's coat with his hair tucked up beneath a braided cap, as we were driven to the Desert Inn in the early hours of the morning.

It must have been a bizarre sight to motorists passing in their air-conditioned cars. There were just the three of us standing by the dusty roadside – people don't walk in Las Vegas unless they are destitute. Lights blazed from every part of the Desert Inn – except for the heavily curtained ninth floor.

'And that's it?' asked John, awe-struck. He was stoned.

'Yeah, that's it,' murmured 'Oiving' 'That's where Howard Hughes lives.'

John stood there silently gazing up, lost in the experience. Someone famous was asleep behind those drapes and no one could reach him. He was untouchable. John didn't express envy. He had no need to.

For days afterwards, he talked about Hughes, quizzing anyone who might know about him. If there was one person John wanted to meet in the whole of America it was no longer Elvis Presley, it was Howard Hughes.

'That would suit me,' he said. 'In one place for ever, instead of all this travelling. Total privacy, nobody to bother you, scream at you, poke your hair or ask what your favourite colour is. I'd just love to meet him and tell him I understand.'

ALL four Beatles were to learn a lot during the '64 summer tour of America and Canada. The first two stops had been an education in themselves. They were to roll across the country playing to an average audience of 12,000 fans a night with the sounds of *Twist And Shout, You Can't Do That, All My Loving, She Loves You, Things We Said Today, Roll Over Beethoven, Can't Buy Me Love, If I Fell, I Want To Hold Your Hand, A Hard Day's Night, Long Tall Sally* and *I Saw Her Standing There*, echoing across the roofs of cities as far apart as Vancouver and Jacksonville. Their support acts included The Righteous Brothers, Jackie de Shannon and the Bill Black Combo.

But there many adventures along the way.

John found good reason to fear for his life and sure enough it was in Dallas. When the Beatles' chartered prop-jet landed, it was directed to a parking position some distance from the terminal after ground controllers warned the pilot that the police could not control 20,000 waiting fans. No sooner had the pilot cut the engines and the aircraft had come to a halt than the crowd broke through the barriers and surged all over the plane. Like an excited swarm, they climbed on to the wings and peered in through the cabin windows.

I was sitting beside John when the captain explained over the intercom that he was powerless to move the plane. Just starting up the engines would mean slicing many Beatle admirers to pieces. 'If someone doesn't do something soon, we'll all be dead,' John told me seriously. 'It only needs one lighted cigarette to get near the fuel tanks and we'll be singing *She Loves You* in Heaven.'

Eventually, a laundry truck was manoeuvred beneath the plane, the Beatles were dropped through the luggage bay into it and driven to the relative safety of their hotel.

***

THE 'Mop Heads' as they had been christened by the American media, arrived in Los Angeles for their concert at that most famous of venues, the Hollywood Bowl, on 23 August. Epstein had been inundated with invitations from the rich and famous who all seemed to want a Beatle (any one of them would do, some even ventured to say) to visit their home for a party.

I had business of my own to attend to in the city. Colonel Parker sent a car to pick me up from the Beverly Hillcrest hotel where I was staying and drive me to his apartment in Westwood for our first face-to-face meeting. And there were to be just two topics of conversation on the agenda: the Beatles and Elvis Presley.

In his first-floor suite at the Beverly Comstock, I found him taking business calls from a hospital bed he used because of an injury to his back. As I arrived, he was just agreeing a deal for the sale of half-a-million framed colour portraits of Elvis – or so he said. The photographs of the Colonel I had seen didn't do him justice. Pale blue eyes and a plump nose sat in a moon-shaped face like ornaments on a pudding, and his ample chins told a story. Yet even semi-crippled, he exuded the ferocity of a rogue elephant, his favourite circus animal.

When he finished making money over the phone, he welcomed me cordially, and I asked him for news of his client.

'Elvis has long wanted to meet the Beatles, but he arranged a while back to spend this break between filming in Memphis,' said the Colonel, ever the diplomat.

Although he had not been out of the apartment for eight weeks, Parker – relying heavily on a walking stick topped with a silver elephant's head – insisted on leaving it to take me down to his offices at the Paramount film studios. Before we left I phoned Epstein, who invited us both to join him for lunch at the Beverly Hills Hotel.

The Presley/Parker memorabilia in his office at Paramount was fascinating, but I was on a mission: how and when were we ever going to be able to get these five superstars together? The Colonel was in no hurry to discuss such a project in. He was keen to point out what he called was an example of what he did – 'promotion'. An illuminated sign above a doorway advertised Elvis's latest picture. The walls of the outer office and the corridors that connected it to the outside world were decorated with Elvis likenesses: billboards for Presley films, advertising material for Presley records, posters for Presley lipstick, handbags and pyjamas. The centrepiece was a cardboard replica of the cellblock in *Jailhouse Rock*.

The walls of his inner room were covered with pictures of Parker with politicians and celebrities: the Colonel with President Lyndon B. Johnson, the Colonel and Elvis with the Speaker of the House, the Colonel with Frank Sinatra. He pointed his cane at the rear wall behind his cluttered desk: 'This here is my dead wall,' he said. 'When anybody dies, I move their picture over here. All these people are deceased.'

Finally we got away and were driven to the Beverly Hills Hotel by the closest thing he'd ever had to an assistant, a former hoofer (vaudeville dancer) by the name of Tom Diskin. To my surprise there were whispers of 'Elvis' and 'Beatles' as the two most famous rock managers in the world shook hands warmly in the foyer. Over lunch, the thing that seemed to concern Brian most was the tight security necessary to protect the Beatles. The Colonel was not impressed.

'You don't have to protect the Beatles the way we protected Elvis because, with them, there is no jealousy,' he snorted. 'You don't have to fear the boyfriends because your artists are characters loved in a different way. The boyfriends would throw things at Elvis on stage. We never had to send in the police to get them – the girls always got 'em first. Your problem is to protect the small fans from getting hurt in the crush. We never had them so little.'

'Will Elvis ever tour again?' Brian asked ignoring the downplaying of his artistes' appeal.

'Put it this way – I'd like him to tour again someday because I'm a showman, but at the moment we can earn more money and entertain more fans by making movies. One day you will discover the same situation with the Beatles.

'Elvis has required every moment of my time, and I think he would have suffered had I signed anyone else, but I admire you, Brian, for doing it your way with other performers as well. Obviously you have a different organisation, but remember, too, that when Presley soared to fame I was 44. When the Beatles happened, you were 28. That helps.'

When the Colonel recalled how he had launched Elvis in the early days by doing rough jobs like selling tickets at dance halls, Brian retorted: 'So did I, in little Lancashire towns. I took around my own posters and sold tickets, but the Beatles were earning less than £20 a show back then. I'm pleased to say things have improved!'

Although the superstars they represented showed little signs of rivalry, the two managers were displaying a high degree of personal one-upmanship.

The following afternoon, which was specially hot and humid, I took the Colonel to meet Messrs Lennon, McCartney, Harrison and Starr. We drove to their rented mansion in Saint Pierre Road, Bel Air, in a station wagon loaded with presents. 'I put on a tie specially for these guys,' said the Colonel.

The Beatles had just finished lunch when we got to the house. Still in trunks after a morning swim, John regarded the Colonel with barely disguised curiosity. I prayed that he wouldn't sabotage the deal I was working hard to piece together.

The Colonel made himself at home at the dining-room table where the remains of lunch were still to be cleared away. He told the group: 'Elvis phoned me this morning to say he was sorry he wasn't here to greet you, but he'd welcome you at

Graceland if you'd like to stop over in Memphis during your tour.'

Ever hopeful, the Beatles discussed the idea, but Brian shook his head with the sort of reluctance he would now adopt to turn down $50,000 deals. 'I don't think our schedule will permit,' he said solemnly. The Colonel shrugged. Secretly, I believe he was relieved. He knew Elvis's state of mind and he himself wasn't physically well enough to deal with his recalcitrant client.

From a large box, the Colonel had brought with him, he handed out his presents like a midsummer Santa Claus. For each of the Beatles, there was a table lamp in the shape of a covered wagon and a leather gun belt – the kind they wore in the western movies of yesteryear. Brian got a gold-coloured one and mine was a silver one spangled with rhinestones (still got it). 'All made specially for you by the guy who made similar stuff for Roy Rogers, the King of the Cowboys,' he boasted.

Ringo put his on and went into the kitchen emerging a few moments later adorned with a cowboy-style hat he'd borrowed from the chef. Somebody produced a cache of imitation six-shooters and the Beatles began a mock gunfight around the dining room. That and the memory of John standing on a Vegas kerb gazing up at Howard Hughes's floor atop the Desert Inn were the most bizarre snapshots I carry in my head from that most extraordinary of summers. 'Bang, bang!' said Paul, aiming his gun at the Colonel. 'You're dead!'

John found a more symbolic target. He pointed his gun at his own head and shouted: 'Bang!'

'I wish we had real guns,' said George.

John caught the implication and frowned.

Was this really happening? Had one of the shrewdest operators in the music business been able to reduce these four famous and talented men to a bunch of junior school boys? Parker didn't hang around to find out. 'And these are from Elvis personally,' he said pointing to a parting gift still in the box from which he'd produced his cowboy souvenirs. Inside were six sets of all the albums Presley had made up to that date. How personal could you get?

'Have fun,' he said. And with that he was gone. Curiouser and curiouser, as Lewis Carroll once wrote.

***

THAT evening, Paul, George and Ringo took up the only 'party' invitation Epstein had accepted on their behalf. They went across to Burt Lancaster's neighbouring mansion to watch Peter Sellers' latest movie, *A Shot in the Dark*. The house was filled with film stars of various vintages, each one keen to see what a Beatle looked like in the flesh.

I stayed at the house with John who was waiting to greet another two of Hollywood's big names – the singer Bobby Darin and his actress wife Sandra Dee. That visit proved uneventful, which is more than could be said when two other people arrived a little later, uninvited. Lennon was sitting in the huge drawing room watching TV and he was bored, but the new arrivals were to prove an entertaining diversion from what was on the box: they were the actress famous for her substantial bosom Jayne Mansfield and a male companion.

'Why, it's *the* Jayne Mansfield,' said John, as though he was really impressed to be greeting the blonde star of *The Girl Can't Help It* which we had all seen several times because Little Richard was in it. 'And Mickey Hargitay,' he said to the complete stranger with her. 'Do come in.'

'Oh, silly,' giggled Jayne, loving it. 'Mickey's my ex. This is my new friend.'

'I'm John,' said the lone Beatle. 'This is Chris. You'll have to make do with us. The others have gone on to a club, the Whiskey-a-Go-Go.'

'Well, let's go and join them,' she giggled again, breathing in deeply.

'No, thanks, I'm staying in,' John responded. 'Would you like a drink?'

'I certainly would. I'll have a cocktail if you can make one,' said Jayne, fluttering her eyelashes.

'I'll get it,' I volunteered. I had never poured a cocktail in my life, but here was my chance to learn. I went into the kitchen and started to examine the bottles. John followed me.

'What do you put in a cocktail?' I asked.

'A drop of that, that, that and that,' he replied, pointing to every liquor bottle on the shelf. 'And then you pee in it.'

I poured gin, vodka, red wine and an unidentified liqueur into a large glass, added ice and handed it to John, who, to my horror, added some liquid Lennon. Jayne pronounced the drink 'a real humdinger' and got even more excited when John told her it was a Beatle Special. Playfully, she tugged John's Beatle haircut and asked: 'Is this real?'

John hated to be touched, particularly by strangers. Dropping his eyes to her enormous bosom, he returned the compliment.

'Are those real?' he asked.

Jayne took a deep breath and replied: 'There's one way to find out.'

Her companion interrupted by flourishing a pack of tarot cards. In return for the hospitality, he said, he would read the cards for John.

'He's going to tell you your destiny . . . and mine,' breathed Jayne, her bosom heaving in John's direction.

None of us knew at this stage that Elvis had been one of Jayne's conquests. She had seduced him after Colonel Parker deliberately demanded an unaffordable fee for him to appear in *The Girl Can't Help It*. The Colonel didn't want Elvis to share billing with Little Richard, Eddie Cochran, Fats Domino and a host of other rock stars. After their one-night stand, Jayne asked Elvis if he would reconsider. 'Ask the

Colonel,' Elvis had yawned. The manager refused to budge, but Elvis gave Jayne a pink motorbike as a consolation prize.

John tolerated the tarot reader while he went through a glib recital of the group's much chronicled success. Then he drew a card that made him stop. He dropped the cards with an expression of mock horror and exclaimed: 'My God, this is terrible. I see an awful ending to all this.'

That was enough for the short-tempered Beatle. John was wildly superstitious and his anger concealed his fear about what fate might have in store for him.

'Out!' he ordered the woman who had briefly once been America's best-known sex symbol, taking her and her companion by the arms and propelling them towards the doorway. His sudden hostility stunned them so much that they went with barely a murmur. Incensed, John turned to me and said we should join the others at the Whiskey-a-Go-Go.

'What a creep that guy was,' he said, relaxing in the car. 'He told me things everyone knows, then tried to scare me witless.'

Getting into the club wasn't easy. News of the Beatles' presence in the popular West Hollywood venue had quickly spreads and a crowd of fans were being manhandled by the police outside. Thankfully, John was by now easily recognizable and we were shoved through the door. Inside, another thousand patrons plus a score of photographers were jostling to join George and Ringo. Paul had found better things to do and had gone off on his own. No sooner was John seated than a familiar voice was heard above the clamour.

'Hi, you guys – fancy seeing you here!'

Jayne Mansfield swanned into view, this time with a photographer in tow and squeezed her skimpily-dressed body into the middle of the group. John tried hard to ignore her but the astute cameraman snapped a picture of three of the Beatles apparently out nightclubbing with Jayne Mansfield. To show his disgust, George flung the remains of his Scotch and Coke at the photographer. An ice cube hit one of the spectators, the actress Mamie van Doren, in the face. As Gentleman George tried to apologise, John whispered to Jayne what had really been in the Beatle Special. A security guard stationed at the table, clutched her arm as she made to strike him and our group made a hasty and undignified exit.

The horribly ironic thing was that the 'phoney' tarot card reader had got it pretty much right. Both John and Jayne died violent deaths, the actress being killed in a car crash in New Orleans only two years later. The next time John and I discussed pre-destination, he remembered that day and worried even more about his future. By this time, he was heavily into numerology under the tutelage of Yoko Ono, and he was obsessed by the number nine, the day of his birth in October 1940.

'Jayne was born on 19 April and she died on 29 June,' he said. 'April is the fourth month and June is the sixth. Add them together and you get ten. I was born on 9 October, the ninth day of the tenth month. She died two months after her birthday, which means I'm going to die on a day with a nine in it, in the month of December.'

* * *

TINSELTOWN was not the only city in which bizarre events occurred. From Cincinnati their chartered plane ferried them in the early hours to New York where they were to play two nights at the Forest Hills Stadium to capacity crowds of 16,000. George Harrison, a nervous flyer at the best of times, was not best pleased to learn that the promoters had decided the safest way to get them into the stadium in the highly condensed district of Queens, would be to drop them in by helicopter.

They had been 'secretly' booked into the Delmonico hotel but yet again the fans were not to be fooled and there were plenty around to witness their 4am arrival. To Ringo's annoyance a girl called Angie McGowan snatched a precious St Christopher medallion from his neck as he made his way into the lobby. Pricked by her conscience, however, she returned it to him at their press conference that afternoon.

The incident did, however, contribute to a tetchy day which was not improved by their late departure for the concert that night. The pilot of the helicopter booked to whisk them across the city's skyscrapers for the show was not given consent for take-off until an hour later than planned. It did not ease George's anxiety and I found myself holding his hand at one point during the flight.

Nevertheless the show was another blazing success and by the time the party returned to the hotel everyone was in high spirits. The group were, as usual, confined to their suite but Neil Aspinall, Mal Evans and I were not subject to the confinement and set off for something we could never have found at home: an all-night picture show. At a cinema off Times Square we sat through more than two hours of *Spartacus*.

Returning in the early hours to the Delmonico, the three of us took the lift to the floor where we had adjacent rooms. Ever-attentive to his charges, Neil headed for the Beatles' suite. Before I could turn the key in the lock of my door, Neil whispered, 'Come and take a look at this'. Through the narrowly opened double doors of their grand rooms, there was a strange sight to behold. Seated on five chairs were John, Paul, George and Ringo with Brian at the end. Every now and again a man standing at the other end would push the closest Beatle off his chair to the next one and in domino effect each would knock the next one off until it reached Brian who would collapse to the floor laughing helplessly, setting the others off.

Neil and I watched this strange game for several minutes – until, that is, we realised who the man doing the pushing from the start of the line was: it was Bob Dylan.

It seems there were more than the six of them in the room but my view from the only partially opened door was confined. However, according to the account of another who I had not seen, that was the night Dylan introduced them to a particularly potent variety of marijuana – far stronger than anything they had sampled before. In fact Mal Evans was always convinced that what they tried for the first time that night was LSD.

I raised the subject with Brian the following day while we were having coffee in his suite. He did not look at all well.

'What was all that about last night?'

'Were you there? I can't remember.'

He popped two amphetamines, washed them down with a glass of water and shivered.

'All I can say about the drug culture is: plenty of drugs but not much culture.'

I finished my coffee and left. I didn't see Brian again for several days and all my enquiries as to his whereabouts were met with mystifying shrugs. Something was not right. It was John who told me what had happened.

'Brian went out the other night and, er, met some fella – a sailor apparently. The guy roughed him up and stole all his

Asprey's gold, his watch, bracelet, pen. He's flown back to London to get replacements.'

'For the whole lot?'

'Yeah. He thinks people will notice they're missing and jump to conclusions, albeit correct ones.'

The image-conscious Brian was normally very cautious about his gay entanglements. But once he had downed a few drinks and partaken of what he called his 'medication', he would seek out rough trade in the low dives around 42nd Street. The confident young impresario, immaculate in Savile Row's finest, would become a giggly, promiscuous fellow.

A psychiatrist once told him that part of his problem was his unrequited love for John Lennon. He was obsessed by John's sardonic wit and artistic genius as well as being attracted by his looks. In many ways, John was the man Brian most wanted to be: he saw the Beatle as being wildly outspoken, incredibly brave and extremely talented.

Sadly for Brian, John was a dedicated womaniser, a veritable conquistador of the opposite sex. The sexual traffic flowing in and out of his hotel bedrooms certainly exceeded that of any of the other Beatles, and his lovers were always female.

John, of course, knew of Brian's lust for him and exploited it to get his own way. They had shared a Spanish holiday in the summer of 1963. Brian told me that in Barcelona he had got no further with John than a single kiss, so he had switched his attentions to a more amenable Spanish bullfighter. John's version was slightly different. He omitted any mention of kissing.

'A lot of rumours floated around about that holiday,' he told me. 'But I just went along with it to try and help Brian's sort his head out. We sat in cafes and talked and talked and talked – mostly about people we'd been in love with. I convinced him that, while I didn't condemn his way of life, I was into women as far as the physical side was concerned.

'I really didn't want to hurt him by saying something stupid like "I can't stand homos." I could understand what was in his head. Anyway, by the end of the holiday, he understood me better and the subject will probably never come up again.'

Brian was convinced that John had never got over the deaths of Stu Sutcliffe and his mother. 'Much of John's anger towards the world is grief over Stu and Julia,' he said. 'He thinks about death a lot.'

***

ONE of my biggest scoops of the tour was to set up a telephone conversation between Paul and Elvis. After they left Los Angeles, the Colonel frequently phoned to keep in touch with the Beatles' progress. When he was unable to get through to the hotel in Atlantic City, he sent a cable asking me to call him urgently. I contacted him on their behalf and he gave me Elvis's private number at Graceland. According to my battered notebook, this was '901 EX(PRESS) 7-4427'. 'You can contact the artist through Marty Lacker,' said Parker, ever wary of eavesdroppers. 'He is waiting for a call from you fellows, so don't let him down.'

I placed the call and once through to the man himself, handed the phone to the closest Beatle to hand: 'How do you do?' enquired Paul in his usual polite manner. 'I want to tell you we all think it's a drag that we weren't able to get together with you, but it's just one of those things. We would still like to meet you if it can be arranged.'

Elvis told Paul that he was disappointed, too. 'I've taken a great big interest in your career and wanted very much to have a long chat with you guys,' he said. 'I've bought an electric bass guitar and I'm learning to play it. The darn thing's given me callouses all over my hand.'

'Well, keep practicing,' said Paul. 'You'll get used to it. When are you coming to England?'

'Soon, I hope. I'm definitely coming.'

'Great! You can count on us having front row seats for your first show.'

'And when are you going to invade the Hollywood studios?' Elvis wanted to know, giving voice to one of his greatest fears.

'Oh, you mean make a film?' answered Paul. 'I don't think we will, really. We like it in Britain and there's no need for us to film in Hollywood, although I appreciate it's the natural thing for an American star to do.'

'Well, I guess you've got a manager to take care of that kind of thing anyway.'

'Too true. I've got no brain for business. I couldn't look after a couple of dollars.'

'Talking of dollars in a pretty modest sort of way, I've bought every single one of your records and we play them all the time up here at the house. I like the cover of your new album (the unsmiling Beatle faces depicted in half light on *With the Beatles*). It's kinda weird and I like weird things. Your faces on that cover remind me of the faces in that movie, *Children of the Damned.*'

This was more like it, a genuine double-edged compliment.

'Talking of films,' said Paul, 'That manager of yours is a laugh. He told us he had an offer from a producer to make a film with both you and us in it. The producer said he was offering a million dollars for Elvis and a million dollars for the Beatles. But Colonel Parker said, "I told him that he had forgotten there were four Beatles and they'd want two million dollars." We thought that dead funny.'

'Yep, that sounds like the Colonel all right,' chuckled Elvis.

At this point, Paul covered the mouthpiece with his hand and said to John: 'Have a word with him, man.'

'No, thanks,' John answered. 'Can't think of anything to say.'

Paul signed off diplomatically and hung up his extension. I took over the conversation. When I asked Elvis about his Beatle collection, he replied: 'I guess I've got every record they ever made here. I'm looking at a copy of *A Hard Day's*

Night right now and I've also hired a copy of the film which we're going to show up here at the house tonight.'

'That's how I spend most of my evenings, watching pictures privately. Coming down to Memphis and just kicking around this house is the only way I get to rest. We have a lot of fun out here. We have some wild parties. It's a pity y'all couldn't have made it over.'

And that was it. The summit meeting the Beatles had hoped for would have to wait for another year. But Paul was happy that contact had been made and I was delighted to be on the inside track.

★ ★ ★

BEFORE the tour ended Brian had one last surprise for his 'boys'. When they had originally agreed the itinerary he had promised them that 17 September would be a rest day. 'I'm afraid that's changed,' he said, 'we will be playing Kansas City that night. The venue is a 20,000-seater.' A loud sigh went up. 'But here's the good news,' he said, 'the promoter is paying a record fee – $150,000 so I'll be able to treat myself to that Rolls Royce.'

'For $150,000,' said George who was already growing suspicious about where all the money was going, 'we should be able to afford one each.'

According to the rock journalist, the late Alfred Aronowitz, who was with Bob Dylan the night he met the Beatles, John, Paul, George and Ringo smoked marijuana that night which he himself provided and that it was the first time they had tried serious pot.

IN THE BEGINNING ... Harrison and Lennon pictured with John's close friend Stuart Sutcliffe. And in the lower picture with Little Richard during their engagement with the legendary American rock and roller at the Star Club in Hamburg.

PUTTING A BRAVE FACE ON IT: After the first night of their UK tour together, Roy Orbison realised that despite his great fame and popularity it was the upstart Beatles who were stealing the show. He gracefully accepted that he would have to take second billing from that point on. Pictured here with them are Gerry and the Pacemakers who were also on the tour.

THE FIFTH BEATLE: Many who tagged along with the group regarded themselves as 'the fifth Beatle' but as Paul McCartney once said, if anyone deserved that label it was their manager Brian Epstein who fought long and hard to turn them into megastars.

Even Prince Philip had to enjoy the joke when three Beatles fought over the single award he presented to them in March 1964.

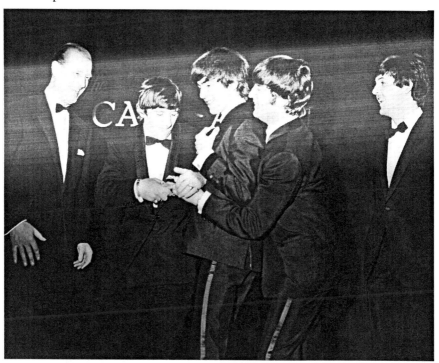

TAKING CARE OF THE MUSICIANS: That's how road managers Neil Aspinall and Mal Evans described their job. An aspiring accountant until he quit his office job to go on the road with John, Paul, George and Ringo, Aspinall later became President of their Apple Corporation. Mal - the bespectacled one - was shot dead in a confrontation with the LAPD.

Once Beatle fans had come to accept that their idols were married men, John and Ringo were able to appear in public with their wives, Cynthia and Maureen.

OFF DUTY: The Beatles were happy to relax with Brian Epstein in their hotel suit after a show. It was a far cry from the shabby flat they called home in their Hamburg days and which the manager said he dreaded visiting.

Paul McCartney courted the actress Jane Asher for five years after they met at author Chris Hutchins' Chelsea flat.

SID BERNSTEIN
PRESENTS THE

BEATLES

IN PERSON

PLUS **ALL STAR SHOW**

SHEA STADIUM

AUG. 15-1965 7:30 P. M.

All Seats Reserved: $4.50, 5.80, 5.75 - Phone 265-2280 For Information

TICKETS NOW AT

THEY HELPED MAKE THE BEATLES, THE BEATLES HELPED MAKE THEM: Sid Bernstein, pictured with Paul, is the man who staged their New York debut concert at Carnegie Hall in February 1964, just three nights after they had appeared on Ed Sullivan's coast-to-coast TV show. They gave Sullivan his highest ever ratings and enterprising Bernstein - who staged their Shea Stadium show the following year - became America's best-known concert promoter after selling all 56,000 tickets for the history-making event.

IS THAT ALL FOR US? The Fab Four, as they became known in the U.S., look down from their hotel balcony as cops struggle to keep the fans from breaking through hurriedly erected barriers. 'We've never seen anything like it,' one policeman told Chris Hutchins. 'Neither have they,' replied the author, 'Neither have they.'

HAVING FUN: Ringo described the four of them as 'brothers - if not closer'. As police sealed off adjacent roads to afford them a few days privacy, John, Paul, George and Ringo (who, like author Hutchins, couldn't swim) splashed happily in the pool of their rented Bel Aire home. It was here that they entertained Elvis Presley's manager, Colonel Tom Parker.

TROUBLE AT THE CLUB: When they did venture out to spend a few hours at the Whiskey-a-go-go club on Sunset Strip, they were descended on by publicity-hungry Jayne Mansfield who had already gate-crashed their Bel Aire house earlier that night. When the actress's boyfriend tried to photograph her with them, George threw his drink at him. He missed but an ice cube hit Mamie van Doren - pictured with George after he had apologised to her. Author Hutchins witnessed it all.

On a visit to the training camp of Muhammad Ali, the world champion boxer had them lie on the floor as he yelled 'You may be the loudest, but I am the greatest!'

new
MUSICAL
EXPRESS

WORLD'S LARGEST CIRCULATION OF ANY MUSIC PAPER

No. 973   EVERY FRIDAY PRICE 6d.   SEPT. 3, 1965   Registered at the G.P.O. as a Newspaper

ELVIS MEETS BEATLES

NME'S
CHRIS
HUTCHINS
WAS THE
ONLY
REPORTER
AT THIS
HISTORIC
EVENT

Read
his
report
on
page
three

THE GREATEST ROCK SUMMIT EVER: By decree of both managers (that's Parker with Presley in his Army uniform) cameras were banned when the Beatles called on Elvis on the night of August 27,1965, but one of the cops guarding the gate of his home, 565 Perugia Way, managed to snap these shots as the party broke up. That's Elvis in the doorway with Chris Hutchins (wearing dark glasses) standing in front of him. And in the picture below that's John Lennon in the white trousers. The meeting was set up by Hutchins but it had unexpected and far-reaching consequences as this book reveals.

LOS ANGELES EVENING AND SUNDAY

HERALD EXAMINER

LARGEST EVENING CIRCULATION IN AMERICA

MONDAY, AUGUST 24, 1964

Beatles Leave L.A. Gasping

RINGO STARR, GEORGE HARRISON, JOHN LENNON (FROM LEFT)
Beatle Harrison points finger, orders photographer not to take picture

BEATLE HARRISON THROWS HIS DRINK AT THE PHOTOGRAPHER
Drink hit the photographer, a deputy sheriff, and actress Mamie Van Doren

FISTFULL OF DOLLARS: On tour the Beatles and their entourage passed much of their time playing cards. On the occasion this photo was taken Chris Hutchins scooped the pot - that's him, third from left back row, waving his winnings in the air. The man in the dark glasses (left, front row) is the Beatles driver Alf Bicknell whose greatest memory of the tour is that Elvis Presley called him 'Sir'.

BAND ON THE RUN: Keeping both the Beatles and their fans safe was a major headache for the organisers of their U.S. tours. The group carried on singing as cops manhandled those who managed to break through the barriers and get on stage. Police in several cities insisted that a condition of them being allowed to perform was that they 'leave town the same night'. During a conversation at the author's flat, Ringo said he feared they could get seriously hurt in such melees. 'Yeah, or seriously rich,' responded John.

SMOKING BUDDIES: The night Bob Dylan came to call on the Beatles in their New York hotel room, he brought with him the rock writer Alfred Aronowitz and he brought with him the strongest dope they had ever tried. Chris Hutchins witnessed the scene as they and Brian Epstein - under Dylan's direction - pushed each other off chairs, giggling helplessly as they did so.

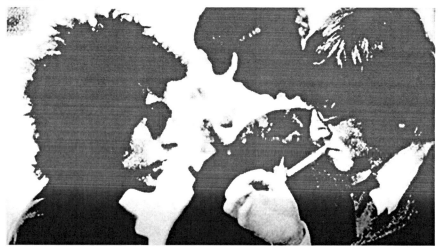

HELLO AND GOODBYE: Happy to pose with manager Epstein early in their meteoric career, John Paul, George and Ringo seemed just as happy in 1968 when they'd agreed to go their separate ways, although it wasn't until April, 1970 that Paul announced it was all over ...

The
BEATLES
★ IN THEIR 1st U. S. CONCERT PERFORMANCE ★

· FEATURING ·

The
Caravelles

Tommy
Roe

The
Chiffons

WASHINGTON SPORTS ARENA
WASHINGTON, D. C.
FEB. 11th - 1964
ALL TICKETS $5.00

26

7

BACK TO BASICS

A FEW weeks after the American tour ended, I got invited back to Kenwood. Once again, John wanted to talk.

First, though, he wanted to listen to some music. While decorators were at work in the main part of the mansion, he and Cynthia were ensconced in a small flat which would eventually be home for their chauffeur and his wife. 'The renovation is costing more than I paid for the bleedin' house,' he said, 'but the money men saying it's increasing the value of the place.'

Once again, it was all so very un-rock 'n roll and his yearning to talk about music with the man from the NME suggested that he was desperate to have a conversation that he could never have with the City wheeler-dealers who were his neighbours.

'Let me play you the Animals' LP – it's great,' he said, adding thoughtfully: 'that's if the record player will work. It gets left on for hours – sometimes all night - and it's a bit burned out.'

We listened to the Animals, and John laughed his throaty chuckle as Eric Burdon broke into his version of *A Hard Day's Night.*

Then, as Cynthia busied herself making tea (where were the booze and the drugs from the Hamburg days of just a couple of years earlier?) it was back to the subject of the house: did it give him the Howard Hughes-style privacy he wanted?

'Sort of,' he said, 'but we get a few "visitors" at the weekend. There's no gate up at the moment. Things will be fine as soon as that little job gets done. George comes around a lot because he only lives a few miles from here. As a matter of fact, I'm expecting him this afternoon with a cat he's giving us.

'This place is well tucked away, but I've bought a car, a Rolls-Royce so I'll be able to get driven up to town whenever the need arises. And Cyn's got a Mini – she's just passed her driving test.'

Domestic bliss, stockbroker style.

'I've never been keen on learning to drive. George, Paul and Ringo have all got high-speed cars now – Paul says he touched 140 mph going up to Liverpool the other day. I'm just not interested in doing that.'

John had been reported as saying he had had enough of globetrotting and would like to settle down in England.

'That's the way I feel at the moment, but I suppose we'll have to go abroad eventually, even if it's only for a holiday. If you could find me somewhere in Britain away from it all, I'd go there. After the Christmas show, we get about a month off, and I suppose Paul and I will have to go somewhere to write the songs for *Help!* But as for settling down, being realistic I don't suppose I could manage that. It's nice to get some peace for a week or two, but after that, it would drive me mad. No, I can't see the Beatles cutting down next year.'

Conversation turned to the group's new record, *I Feel Fine*. 'I actually wrote it around that riff going on in the background. I tried to get the same effect into practically every song on the album, but the others wouldn't have it. I told them I'd write a song specially for that riff, so Paul and George said, "Yeah, you go away and do that," knowing that we had almost finished the album. Anyway, going into the studio one morning, I said to Ringo, "I've written this song but it's lousy." Anyway, we tried it, complete with the riff, and it sounded like an A-side, so we agreed to go with it, just like that.'

It was turning into too much of a music paper interview so John decided it was time for another look around the house. He'd painted Julian's bedroom bright red and pointed out that his son even had his own bathroom. Another bedroom was decorated blue and Cynthia had reserved it for any additions to the family, although John said such an event was unlikely. He was growing maudlin. They had knocked two rooms into one to create a new super master bedroom at the front of the house but the choice of sage-green walls suggested this was no love chamber.

The room he seemed happiest about was his study; one he boasted was 'my own private room. I get left alone in here'. Decorated in scarlet, it was the only dramatic area in the house.

Not waiting for George to arrive with the cat, I left the house feeling vaguely disturbed. Could this last? Could the marriage last? Back in my own home, I called Bill Harry, who was the publisher of *Mersey Beat* and the writer who had known the Beatles longest.

'I could never imagine John as Squire Lennon sitting in a nice house admiring the garden,' said Bill. 'From the first time I met him, he was always looking for something. He was a seeker. At art college, John, Stuart [Sutcliffe] and I talked about metaphysical things like the meaning of life, astral travel and mystical dimensions. We talked about how the philosopher's stone wasn't about the transformation of base metal into gold, but rather a code that the alchemists had for the evolution of man.

'John and I got on extremely well because we were rather tougher than other people. John used to humiliate Stuart and put him down because it was in his nature to take advantage and dominate other people if he could. But if you stood up to him, he would back down. He was a lot more intelligent than people gave him credit for. His Aunt Mimi used to phone me and say, "I will always remember you, Bill, because you were the first one to call John a genius."

'He had this talent as an artist, but he didn't really have proper art tuition. He got expelled from art college because of his wild reputation. So, all his lines and illustrations came from within himself. He was self-taught.

'After I published his article "The Dubious Origins of the Beatles", he was so chuffed that he came round to the office with this big bundle of stuff. It was nearly everything he had ever written or drawn: 250 drawings, stories about Small Stan and *The Tale of Hermit Fred*, amazing poems. They were fascinating. He had done all these wicked satires of political figures of the day like Prime Minister Macmillan. I crammed a whole drawer with them and told him I was going to print some in every issue of *Mersey Beat*. I told him I'd run a column called "Beatcomber" because I liked Beachcomber in the *Sunday Express*.

'So I started publishing John's column, and then *Mersey Beat* got so successful, we had to move. We'd started in this tiny attic and now we needed a whole floor of the building. My wife Virginia did the moving while I was out doing an interview. When I opened the drawer to get John's new thing out there was nothing in there. Virginia had thought it was all rubbish and had thrown it in the bin. The dustmen had taken the lot.

'I knew John would go bananas, but I had to tell him, so that night we went down to the Blue Angel – a local nightclub - and John was there. He cried on Virginia's shoulder.

'John always believed he was frustrated – he had all this creativity within him, but he lacked somebody to recognise it and draw it out of him. He needed to channel his work through a sponsor or a patron. Instead, he found his way into drink and drugs. He liked to think through drink; he believed that being a big drinker would enable him to write better and do things better.

'Then it was on to drugs. The first time he got into drugs was in Liverpool when this poet came back with him to his flat in Gambier Terrace and broke open a Vick's inhaler: he had Benzedrine in there and John just chewed the raw Benzedrine.

'When John went over to Hamburg, he got Prellies, which you could buy over the counter at the chemist's; they made you high. Then he moved on to other things and eventually LSD, which helped him to write those songs. But he was still looking for answers.

'He's always trying to find the creative thing. What he really needs is someone to give him a kick up the bum.'

When a newspaper report appeared suggesting that the Lennon marriage to Cynthia was in trouble, I got a message from John asking me to write a piece stating that all was fine. I didn't do it; I didn't believe him.

8

ON THE ROAD IN '65

DURING the bitterly cold winter of 1965, the young of New York knew what they wanted: the return of the Beatles. As he had trudged through the sidewalk slush to reach his apartment at 12th Street and 6th, Sid Bernstein resolved to give them just that.

In his mind, he had conceived the greatest rock event since David slew Goliath. Not only would he bring the Beatles to New York again, but he would play them at the city's biggest venue, Shea Stadium. Shea, home of the Mets baseball team, right beside La Guardia Airport in Queens, could hold a capacity crowd of 55,600. There was only one minor detail stopping him: once again he was completely broke. But the fact that he owed rent to his landlord and couldn't afford to pay his grocer's bill was a mere trifle compared with the magnificence of his scheme. It was Sunday 10 January 1965, and Sid shook the snow off his boots, picked up the phone and once again called Brian Epstein.

As delighted as he was to hear from the promoter who had masterminded the Beatles' two concerts at Carnegie Hall, Brian was sceptical when Sid mentioned Shea. He became more amenable after Sid offered to recompense him for every unsold seat in the house.

'Brian told me he'd be at the Waldorf in three months' time, and added, "Please don't advertise or publicise the fact that you have got the Beatles until you've given me a $50,000 deposit. Will you do me that favour?" I agreed, but asked him if I could tell my friends. He said, "I can't stop you talking to your friends."'

Sid was grateful for small mercies. He had a deal even if he couldn't announce it in the press. 'I had just lost an awful lot of money on a road show version of the TV series Shindig, which featured Gerry and the Pacemakers (another Epstein group), and a number of American rock'n'roll artists. But the kids in my neighbourhood knew that I'd brought the Beatles to New York in 1964 and they used to talk to me. I lived in Greenwich Village, right outside Washington Square Park, which is a big hangout place for kids. I used to take my only child at that time – Adam who was 1-year-old – to the park. Kids would ask me, "What's next, Mr Bernstein, who's coming next?" I had something to tell them that Sunday and they went wild: The Beatles at Shea Stadium!

'I decided, after that reaction, to get a post office box six blocks from my home. I took out PO Box 21, told a few more kids, mentioned the price of the tickets, and waited three weeks. I was desperate. If I got fifty letters, I could pay my rent, if it was sixty or seventy I could pay my grocery bill.

'The post office was open until 1.00 pm on Saturday, and walking the six blocks from my house, I arrived at 12.15. When I got there, I found I'd forgotten my post box key. I went up to the enquiry desk and I told the guy I had a box here, but no key. As they were closing soon, could he open it for me? I showed him my driver's licence for identification, and he said, "You're Sid Bernstein, Box 21?" I said, "Yes," and he said, "What's your racket, buddy?" I told him, "I'm in the mail order business," and he said, "You must have some hot item." He pulled out three of the biggest duffel bags I'd ever seen. I shot back real fast to get my car and took those three huge sacks to my home.

'On 10 April, I called the Waldorf and got connected to Brian. "Welcome to New York," I said. "If you have time to see me, I've got the deposit for you." We had banked

$185,000 and were still counting. In those three weeks, the grapevine had told the world. There were letters from Japan, Italy, Scandinavia, England, South America and most of the fifty states. We had to send back 100,000 letters and we hadn't placed a single advertisement.'

By the time summer arrived, a Shea ticket was the hottest item on the black market.

***

BEING up close and personal to the Beatles was getting me acres of space in the *NME*, but I still yearned for the big story. More hopeful, after hearing the invitation to visit Graceland from the King's own lips, I kept in touch with the Colonel until the Beatles returned to the US in August 1965. This was the year that the Queen awarded them MBEs for services to Britain's export drive. Some outraged holders of the award promptly sent their medals back to Buckingham Palace, one pompous Canadian MP saying that he refused to be placed on the same level as 'vulgar nincompoops' When the Queen asked the Beatles at the investiture: 'How long have you been together?' Ringo replied: 'About forty years, ma'am.' It just seemed like that to him.

In any event John, the anti-war campaigner, found the idea of medals of any kind repellent. He later claimed that he smoked dope in the Palace loo to express his true feelings and he eventually disowned his honour. 'I thought you were supposed to do something brave in war to get one of these,' he told me. 'Well, there's never been any chance of me doing that. This is just a political gimmick to make [the Prime Minister] Harold Wilson look good.'

More important to John was the fact that in March 1965 President Lyndon B. Johnson had sent 3,500 US Marines into Da Nang, the first American fighting troops to be committed to the field in South Vietnam. He hated war in general and Vietnam in particular. When Johnson announced at the end of July that he had decided to send in another 50,000 troops, John burst out: 'Who does he think he's kidding? That was the idea all along.'

John almost sabotaged Sid Bernstein's dream by threatening to stage a one-Beatle boycott of the States, but luckily for me, he packed his bags along with the rest of us. We flew to

New York on TWA flight 703. The date was Friday the 13th. I kept my fingers crossed.

That day the Beatles took up residence as the sole occupants of the 33rd floor of the Warwick Hotel on the corner of 54th Street and 6th, not far from PO Box 21. Any thoughts they might have had of setting foot outside were soon abandoned. The New York Police Department had learned from events of the previous summer that the only way they could protect the Beatles was to imprison them. The night we arrived the group had to cancel plans to go to the Copacabana to see the Supremes.

None of us could quite comprehend what lay in store at Shea. 'I suppose it will be like any other concert, only louder,' said Ringo, pacing around the suite.

John was in a reflective mood.

'I guess this is the turning point,' he said. 'How do you follow Shea?'

He turned up the TV sound to listen to the news. The headlines were focussed on race riots, which were ripping through the ghettoes of Los Angeles. The army had been sent in.

'Unbelievable – Johnson sends 50,000 troops to Vietnam, but there's a war going on in his own country,' said John. 'I'm glad I just play music.'

Mick Jagger and Keith Richard, who had become good friends with the Beatles, were also in New York, with their manager Andrew Oldham, and they invited me to travel to Shea with them for the mega-concert. We went in a yacht called *Princess*, which either belonged to or was chartered by (we never could work out which) the Stones' American lawyer Allen Klein. Joined by the singer Brian Hyland we were photographed before casting off by an enthusiastic young female photographer who made it clear she was very keen on rock stars. Her name was Linda Eastman and, of course, she later became Mrs Paul McCartney.

I talked to the Beatles over the yacht's radio-telephone as they prepared for the biggest event of their lives. Mick chatted to George Harrison about plans for that evening, to take his mind off the concert. Talking through the hotel switchboard, George gave Mick the hush-hush number of a private line to the Beatles' suite. What he didn't realize, however, was that 2,000 other vessels in the Hudson River basin had tuned in. Needless to say, that private number was jammed for the rest of their stay in New York.

Lazing on deck in the summer sunshine, Mick told me: 'I don't envy the Beatles. Look how much freedom we have and they're locked up in their hotel bedrooms without even being able to take a car ride, let alone do something like this.'

Then he played Bob Dylan's latest single – 'pressed secretly for us eager maniacs' – and danced on deck in the androgynous style that identifies him on stage. Later, I joined him on the bridge where he was involved in a serious conversation about 'the Brian Jones problem'. Mick wanted the Stones' founder and original leader out of the band.

At 5pm, *Princess* sailed under the Queensboro Bridge and headed up the East River towards Flushing Bay.

As the yacht berthed almost in Shea's shadow, we learned that a radio station had monitored the phone call with George and broadcast the Stones' plan to tie up near the stadium. Hundreds of fans locked out of the concert were waiting in ambush. Jagger and co had to run ashore and jump into a waiting car, which rushed the party into the stadium where we were hit by a wall of sound. Ringo had been right: it was louder: the roar of the crowd was like a dozen jet fighters taking off simultaneously.

'This is frightening,' exclaimed Jagger.

'It's bloody deafening,' yelled Keith Richard.

And they were only warming up.

The five of us dashed in through the artists' entrance and met up with the Beatles, who were about to go on stage. They had been flown to Queens in a helicopter and loaded like bullion into a Wells Fargo security van for safe delivery. Sid Bernstein was taking no chances. To him they were bullion.

'It's the famous Stones,' yelled John.

'Who are these people?' demanded an irate cop.

'They're the same as the Beatles,' roared John.

'I don't care who they are,' the cop roared back. 'They can't stand in the aisle. There's a fire regulation.'

'Then put it out,' jested George.

The cop relented just as the Beatles were due to go on stage. They had to run across the baseball diamond to the rostrum in its centre. Everyone knew beforehand that this had to be the greatest Beatle concert of all time, but nothing could have prepared any of us for the pandemonium that broke out when the Beatles came into view.

Ed Sullivan, compere for the event, announced: 'Now, ladies and gentlemen, honoured by their country, decorated by their Queen and loved here in America: Here are the Beatles!' If the stadium had had a roof, it would have been blown sky-high. Never have I heard such a blast. The screaming, shouting, whistling and stomping swelled into a crescendo that sent me and the Stones reeling backwards in the aisle. The Beatles had literally rolled the Stones.

As Paul kicked off with *Twist and Shout*, the fevered excitement rose even higher and the noise increased in volume with each offering until all I was aware of was a dull, throbbing ache. It reached a peak when John played a keyboard with his elbow in *I'm Down*. Fans broke through the 2,000-strong police cordon around the edges of the diamond, only to be brought down in tackles by a second line of defence nearer the stage.

'I've never felt so exhilarated in my life,' said George when the group collapsed back at the Warwick. 'It was unbelievable, so many people wanted to see us.'

'It would have been better still if we could have heard what we were playing,' said John. 'I wasn't sure even what key I was in on two numbers.'

No one was really complaining. For a single concert, the Beatles received $160,000 out of a box-office total of $304,000. After he had paid everyone connected with the show, including $25,000 to Lloyd's of London for insurance, Sid Bernstein's profit was just $6,500, his lucky number. He did, however, manage to pay both his rent and the grocery bill that week.

***

AS the tour progressed that summer, I noticed that John was becoming less frightened and more frivolous. Staying stoned most of the time helped him to cope with the danger, such as the incident that happened during our flight to Portland, Oregon, in a four-engine Lockheed Electra. The plane flew through a gorge with towering rocks reaching into the clouds above.

'Do you see anywhere we could land if we had to?' Paul asked nervously.

A game of blackjack was in progress at the time and I was winning. There was a large pile of dollar bills in front of me as I dealt the cards.

'Oi, look! shouted George, pointing disbelievingly out of the window. 'The bleedin' thing's on fire!'

'Stop playing games and play cards,' I snapped, continuing to deal. George had been nervous of flying ever since a window beside him had burst open while a small plane taking the Beatles from Liverpool to London had been hurtling down the runway. Terrified of being sucked out, George had called for help, and, just in time, an air stewardess had stopped the pilot from taking off.

Nor was George kidding this time. The Electra's port engine was indeed spitting flames. Dollar bills and playing cards flew into the air. The seatbelt warning sign flashed on with urgent pings. A stewardess checked the belts were fastened. I looked at George. He was in a state of nervous collapse. He undid his belt, got up and stood by the emergency exit, anxious to be the first out when we landed. 'Now perhaps people will stop joking about how long we're going to last,' he said seriously.

I looked at John to see how he was taking this, and he stared calmly back. Only John, once again revealing his macabre disposition towards death, could see the funny side.

'When this thing gets down,' he shouted to the stewardess, 'it's Beatles and children first!' Needless to say, the aircraft landed safely.

Following the Beatles' two concerts at the Portland Coliseum, the Beatles' circus took off for Los Angeles at midnight in a replacement plane. We landed at LAX in the early hours of Monday 23 August for a nine-day stay. I knew I wasn't going to get much sleep. Elvis was in town; it had to be now or never.

***

MY friendship with Colonel Tom Parker was resumed within hours of my arrival in what he called 'his town' (although I learned later that he was an illegal Dutch immigrant and his real name was Andreas Cornelius von Kujik). My number one priority was to set up that meeting for the Beatles with Presley and I had no difficulty hooking up with the megastar's manager since he had an insatiable appetite for information about the opposition – the boys from Liverpool.

We drifted into the same routine as we had had the previous summer: he would call at my hotel each morning – always wearing a short-sleeve beach shirt, slacks and a white panama hat and clutching a cane topped with a silver elephant's head – always with Tom Diskin at the wheel of the station wagon, he would take me to his office at Paramount Studios and there I was obliged to stay for most of the day. By now I was growing impatient and nagged him incessantly. 'When can I meet Elvis?' I'd ask over and over again, knowing that such a meeting was imperative if I was going to get him in the same room as John, Paul, George and Ringo. Each time he would reply wearily, 'How many times have I gotta tell you son? Mr Presley don't talk to the press. No exceptions.' Then he would bombard me with more questions about the group: how much was Brian getting for each gig? What commission were the agents taking? What were the concession deals? He was big on the latter: he had made a fortune out of cheap

Elvis souvenirs sold outside the concert venues and even donned a white coat to man the stands himself. To him, merchandise meant more than music.

Just a few days later we were walking to lunch at the studio restaurant complex when he said he had to make a slight detour to drop off some papers. Like all studios, the Paramount lot was a curious amalgam of vast sound stages, office buildings and idiosyncratic houses where writers and directors work and stars rest between shoots. We stopped at one of these and the Colonel motioned me to take a seat as he went to see someone upstairs. As I had stepped out of brilliant sunshine into a dimly lit room, it took more than a few moments to get accustomed to the gloom. When I did, I became aware that I was not alone and almost immediately I realised that the figure sitting just a few feet away from me was Elvis Presley. The man himself. I was, after all then, an exception to his manager's rule.

Ever a courteous gentleman, Elvis – wearing a green bolero shirt with puffed sleeves and tight black slacks and shiny black boots studded in silver – stood up to shake hands. Given the scale of the build-up to this moment, it was probably inevitable that I would fluff my lines and I suspect that most of what I came out with was drivel, but I remember well his opening gambit. 'You're the guy travelling with the Beatles I talked to on the phone last year. I hear you want me to meet 'em.' So nervous at the prospect of him saying 'no', I simply nodded my reply. 'What are they like? What's Lennon like?' Clearly curious about the four who had taken the world by such storm, he said he'd had his girlfriend drive by their rented house to assess the situation. 'She said there were a heck of a lot of fans outside,' he added. I wasn't sure whether he thought that was good or bad.

'What you really want is a story for your newspaper,' he said, breaking into a broad grin. I told him that was not strictly true. John, Paul, George, Ringo and I were friends and they had made it a challenge for me in Hamburg three years earlier to try and set up a meeting with a man we all regarded as the King. He nodded acceptance and said he wanted to know more about John. 'I hear he's a fag. Is that right?'

'No,' I replied, explaining that the story emanated from an incident I witnessed when John stepped outside his motel room during a stop on the previous tour and asked a cop standing guard if he could get him some fags. 'He meant cigarettes,' I told Elvis. 'That's what we call them in England.'

He shook his head. 'English sure is a weird language. So how good is this John Lennon? Could he have made it on his own?'

I could see where he was going. 'He's a bright guy,' I replied, 'very bright. But the Beatles are a group. They'd be the first to admit that individually none of them could have achieved the success that you've done on your own. If you'd agree to meet them, you'd find they're okay guys.'

His next remark gave me an insight into how powerful his manager was when it came to manipulating his thinking.

'The Colonel says their manager just wants the publicity so they can boast about knocking me off my perch.'

'No, I promise you the meeting was my idea. As I said, we've been talking about it since long before they became famous. They still can't believe what's happening to them.'

'Yeah, I can identify with that. It happens so fast it takes your breath away.'

'Will you do it? Will you meet them?'

He shrugged. 'Depends. I'll do whatever the Colonel recommends. He hasn't been wrong so far, though sometimes I wonder… It would be good to go back on the road and do what the Beatles are doing but I wouldn't do it without the Colonel – never have, never will and he can't do it. His back hurts pretty bad, and he thinks he would crack up before a tour was half completed.'

Then, as if on cue (I wondered afterwards if he had been listening-in to the conversation), the Colonel came back down the stairs and, without a word to Elvis, said to me, 'Come on, let's go get that lunch.' As we walked outside, I was keen to thank him for setting up such a memorable meeting but he was having none of it. Staring straight ahead, his teeth clenched on a cigar, he said woodenly, 'Mr Presley? I didn't see no Mr Presley.' It must have been hard for him to break his life-long rule of keeping Elvis and journalists apart and he was clearly not keen to admit that he had just broken a cardinal rule.

Over lunch I asked him yet again if we were going to arrange a meeting between Elvis, John, Paul, George and Ringo. He said he would need to discuss the matter with Brian. Later that afternoon, after he'd taken me on the set to be photographed with Elvis, I escorted him up to the house for his second meeting with the Beatles.

In their rented house at 2850 Benedict Canyon above Beverly Hills, they probed him, yet again, about Elvis's career. Why wasn't he doing what they were doing? He gave them much the same answer Presley had given me a few hours earlier: 'Elvis is unavailable for personal appearances because of his film commitments.' It sounded pompous, boastful even when he added: 'I've just sent his gold Cadillac on a tour of Australia. Matter of fact, it's so successful I'm thinking of putting his gold suit on tour.'

When, after an hour, he announced he was leaving, the Colonel assured the Beatles that they would meet Elvis, subject to me being able to fix a convenient time and place. This was good news. It was all down to me.

The following day I got the two managers together to thrash out the arrangements. Parker and I circled the pool at the Beverly Hills Hotel until we located Brian, clad in swimming trunks and a white toweling robe, straddling a Li-lo outside the cabana he had rented for the week. To my relief, his fresh, babyish face coloured red by the West Coast sun, Brian looked happy and relaxed. The Colonel grasped his outstretched hand and said: 'Okay, let's work something out.'

Lunch was served poolside. Brian and I ate lobster salad and drank chilled Chablis. 'One of life's little pleasures,' Brian said, mixing his own salad dressing from stoppered bottles of olive oil and vinegar.

The Colonel chose chicken: 'I'm mighty partial to chicken. I started out with this little [circus] sideshow – dancing chickens. Now chickens are not by nature Fred Astaire, so how did I make' em dance?' I'd heard the story before – more than once. 'Well, Brian, you'd dance if you were standing on a hotplate, a little fire underneath it. I'd start each week with seven dancin' chickens and finish with just one.' He flourished a chicken leg. 'Well, a fella's gotta eat!'

The Colonel laughed heartily at his own jokes. Brian frowned. Never had the gap between their cultures seemed wider. Realising he had failed to amuse the businessman from Liverpool, Parker turned serious: 'Let's get down to logistics.'

'As you know, Colonel, the boys are staying in Benedict Canyon,' Brian began.

'Yeah, I've been up there to take a look. Could present security problems.'

'There are going to be security problems wherever they meet,' Brian replied, colouring visibly. He liked to get his own way as much as the Colonel.

'Mr Presley lives in a secure part of Bel Air.'

'So you're insisting that we visit you.'

'"Insist" is a strong word. Listen, Brian (he had a bit of a problem with his r's so it always came out as 'Bwian', you're in our country so we must be the hosts. If Mr Presley were in your homeland, we'd come to you. That's the way of it.'

'You have a point. OK. I've got to go to New York but I'll be back on Friday. What about Friday night?

The Colonel whipped out a diary and scribbled a note in it. 'Friday night it is. August 27.' He snapped the dairy shut and pocketed it. 'Only one stipulation. No publicity – apart from what Chris here writes for his newspaper after the event.'

'That's going to be tricky, Colonel,' said Brian. 'Fleet Street is here in force. They'll go crazy.'

The Colonel turned to me. 'That's your job. Lay down a false trail. Give the competition the slip.'

I nodded my assent: 'Leave it to me.' Of all the stories in my short, though busy, career, this was the one I most wanted to myself.

Ever the tough negotiator, Parker wasn't finished: 'And another thing. No cameras, no pictures of any kind and no tape-recorders. That agreed?' He offered his hand to the man who managed the Beatles.

'Anything else?' asked Brian, failing to disguise his irritation but shaking the Colonel's hand before it was withdrawn. 'By the way, Colonel, what is Mr Presley's address in Bel Air?'

Caught unprepared, the Colonel blustered: 'That will have to remain classified information. I'll send one of my men to pick your boys up.'

'That's ridiculous,' Brian exclaimed. I wasn't about to tell him that since Parker and Presley rarely socialised, he probably didn't know the address.

Parker rose abruptly to his feet. 'If that's the way you feel, I'd as soon call the whole damn thing off, only we've shaken on it. Anyway, I'm doing this as a personal favour to my friend Mr Hutchins here.'

I jumped up and reassured him: 'I'm sure we'll manage, Colonel. It will be all right on the night.'

***

BACK at 2850 Benedict Canyon, a strange silence prevailed when Brian gave them news of the meeting. They had waited so long that it seemed too good to be true. 'I bet he cancels,' said John sourly. He listened to the account of my audience with the King, and even though I omitted the personal references that Elvis had made about him, he professed to be unimpressed.

'I'm fed up with meeting celebrities,' he said wearily. 'Most of them are disappointing, and I bet he's going to be the same.'

I knew what was bugging him. The day after their arrival in LA, the Beatles had attended a party hosted in their honour at the Capitol Records Tower in Hollywood. The venue was carpeted wall-to-wall be some of the best known people in Tinseltown. Those I recognised included Steve McQueen, Julie Andrews, Richard Chamberlain, James Stewart, Rock Hudson, Gene Kelly, Edward G. Robinson and Jane Fonda. Once again, though, John, Paul, George and Ringo were displayed as novelties rather than real people in their own right.

***

NOTHING, however, nothing was going to spoil the plan for Friday night. When Brian left for his business trip to New York, I made sure I stuck close to his boys. Captive in Benedict Canyon, life revolved around the swimming pool and the games room. Neither Ringo nor I could swim but we both tried to learn a few strokes in the pool. John borrowed my camera and took some holiday snaps of Paul wearing Mal's glasses as a nervous Ringo surveyed the deep end. We played pool in the games room, Ringo deliberately using the blunt end of the cue. 'This is Ringo time at the table,' he said when someone pointed out his mistake. 'I play my way.' Was he trying to grow more assertive or was there rebellion in the air? The photographs taken may have looked like happy holiday snaps but there was definitely tension in the air.

I did part company with the Beatles on the eve of the summit meeting. While they went off to a recording studio to watch their folk-rocking friends the Byrds record Bob

Dylan's latest offering, *The Times They Are A-Changing*, I answered a summons from the Colonel to join him on a reconnaissance mission apparently to ensure that the most expedient route to Elvis's house was worked out. At least that's how he put it: I learned on the trip that what I had guessed when he refused to give Brian the address was correct. He didn't know it: he had never actually been to Elvis's home. They didn't socialise, he had little or nothing to do with Elvis's music and he made deals for poor films but what's important is that without this master of management, Elvis might never have been discovered, the world might never have known about him. Thank God then, for Colonel Parker.

'Just carry on up this hill, Mr Diskin,' he instructed his mild-mannered and obliging assistant at the wheel of the shooting brake. 'Let's see, Bellagio Road. Every goddam street around here is Bellagio. It's up here some place. We want Perugia Way, number 565.' Consulting a road map of the area, I located Perugia Way at the top of Bellagio overlooking the Bel Air Country Club.

'Ah, yes, the country club,' lied the Colonel. 'I remember now.'

Finally, the wagon pulled up on the crest of a steep hill outside the high-security gates of 565 Perugia Way. A Rolls-Royce, two Cadillacs and three Harley-Davidson motorcycles were parked in the driveway under a row of palm trees. The courtyard leading up to a panelled front door was lushly planted with petunias, tiny hedges, a profusion of ferns and strips of well-tended lawn. The house, a two-storey mansion, was built into the hillside. Most of it was hidden from the roadway by bowed garden walls seven feet high, covered in tropical creepers.

'All right, Mr Diskin,' the Colonel ordered. 'Let's head back to civilisation.'

I had hoped to go inside, and said so. The Colonel, however, had a management rule to cover just such an eventuality: 'Never interfere with the client's private life. Mr Presley leads his life and I lead mine. We're strictly business. Friday is business and this is Thursday.'

And with that we drove back down to the more familiar territory of Beverly Hills.

'The Colonel is a wily old fox,' Liberace's manager Seymour Heller told me later. 'He didn't get too close because – and here's the truth of the matter - he didn't like a lot of the things that Elvis did, drugs or whatever, and he didn't like his friends.'

After they subsequently announced their retirement from touring, Sid Bernstein placed a full page newspaper advertisement offering the Beatles a million dollars to do one more live concert. They never responded. Bernstein died in August 2013 aged 95.

9

THE BEATLES MEET ELVIS

FRIDAY night, 27 August 1965. The bar of the Beverly Hillcrest Hotel was crowded with newshounds in search of an exclusive. It was already early Saturday morning in London and the big Sunday newspapers would soon be screaming for some action on the Beatle front.

I was drinking alone, keeping the biggest secret of my life carefully under wraps. My friend Don Short, a reporter with the *Daily Mirror*, detached himself from one group and, drink in hand, joined me. 'Porky' Short was a chubby, prematurely balding man with the glow of a relentless bon vivant. But he had a wicked news sense and he sensed that something was up.

'I've spoken to Brian,' he said, leaning into the bar to suggest confidentiality. 'Something's going on. He wouldn't tell me what. It's Elvis, isn't it? Elvis meeting the Beatles?'

'Brian's in New York,' I replied. 'Anyway, why ask me? If I knew anything like that, I wouldn't be sitting here, would I?'

'I'm asking you because you're in with Brian and the Colonel. Come on, Chris. Remember, we're pals.'

I knew there was only one way out of this corner: 'Okay, okay. Just keep it to yourself, right? Elvis is meeting the Beatles tonight. But security is tight. I can't get you in. You'll have to find your own way.'

'Just give me the address.'

I levered myself off the bar stool, whipped out a pen and scribbled on the back of my bar check.

'Pick up my tab. If anyone asks, I've gone to the movies.' As I left, I secretly hoped that Porky enjoyed the striptease show at the address I'd copied down from a board above the bar payphone.

Parker collected me from the back of the hotel and we headed for LAX to pick up Brian Epstein on his return from New York. His flight arrived on time and he was soon aboard Parker's station wagon with Tom Diskin at the wheel. There was an ominous silence in the vehicle as Diskin swung it on to the San Diego Freeway. The Colonel broke it by asking Brian: 'Everything set your end?'

'Well, it was when I left New York,' was the tetchy reply.

'Just checkin',' said the Colonel, clearly enjoying the fact that he was now in charge. Through the windscreen, a street sign read 'SUNSET BLVD'.

'We change cars here,' commanded the Colonel. Everyone piled into a white limousine parked beside the kerb. When we reached Benedict Canyon, we switched cars again, this time into a black limousine with one of the Memphis Mafia at the wheel.

'Sure you weren't followed?' demanded the Colonel.

'Not unless they're hiding in the trunk,' the Mafioso answered sourly.

'Go check,' remonstrated the Colonel. 'We can't be too careful.'

The limousine swept past cops looking out for intruders until it reached the five-bar gate which marked the entrance to No. 2850, Mulholland Drive, Benedict Canyon. Already alerted to the news that the managers were on their way, we watched as John, Paul, George and Ringo emerged from the house and climbed into the back of their own limousine driven by Alf Bicknell, the British chauffeur who had accompanied them to America. Thoroughly enjoying the intrigue, the Colonel shouted like a wagon master: 'Roll 'em!'

Parker's alert to the LAPD, who already had adjacent roads closed to all but those who could prove they were residents while the Beatles were holed up in the Canyon, proved effective. Police motorcycles pulled into the road to prevent anyone from following the limousines with their precious cargo, and moved ahead to block roads at approaching junctions in order to allow the vehicles to proceed without having to pause.

Halfway down the Canyon, the motorcade veered off to the right rejoining Sunset Boulevard near the iconic stone archway into Bel Air.

More police cars blocked the roadway, holding up traffic. Red lights flashed and the crackle of police radios sounded in the night. Then the road started to curve and rise steeply. This journey had been uphill all the way. Now, I was praying it would be a smooth ride back down.

***

A SHORT driveway off Perguia Way – part of the highly-exclusive Bel Air Country Club Estate – led to the grand front entrance of number 565. The white painted house was spectacularly floodlit seemingly in preparation for the great event it was to host on this balmy summer evening. I watched as the four boys from Liverpool – three from council house homes – stepped from their limousine to stand and stare at the elegant property before them. Perhaps, I wondered, Elvis had felt the same when he first viewed it. After all, he had been raised in a two-room shack in the one-horse town of Tupelo, Mississippi with no indoor bathroom, and this house had several. All five men had come such a long way and never was it more clear than at this moment.

As the electronically controlled wrought iron gates closed silently behind us, our group finally moved towards two towering palm trees guarding the front door where Elvis's main man, the ebullient Joe Esposito, stood waiting to greet his boss's guests. The large diamond set in the ring on his left hand (a gift from Elvis), glittered in the bright lights as he shook hands with each of us. After some brief banter with Colonel Parker – this man, after all, had to serve two masters

– he led us into a two-storey entrance hall which featured a magnificent double staircase. This was luxury living at its finest. Early in 2015 the house was on the market for $18.5 million.

I patted the breast pocket of my jacket to make sure I had not forgotten the notebook in which I would secretly record (on frequent visits to the loo!) the fine detail of what I saw and heard over the next few hours. Missing for many years, that notebook recently resurfaced during a house move of my own and allows me access to information I had previously failed to recall. Needless to say it is now stored in a safe with other valuables such as the postcard reproduced on the cover of this book and some historic letters from both Brian Epstein and Colonel Parker.

By now John, Paul, George and Ringo were surrounded by the Memphis Mafia – the men from Tennessee who made up Elvis's Praetorian Guard. I caught John's eye and for once he looked as though he didn't know how he should behave: this was not the world of rock'n'roll he was expecting. I was about to offer him some reassurance when the ever-smiling Esposito delivered the dramatic invitation the Beatles had waited so long to hear: 'Come and meet Elvis'.

And with that he led the group into a vast living room where The King, smiling broadly, rose from his place on a horseshoe couch. Suntanned and seemingly relaxed – although looks could be deceiving – he was wearing a scarlet shirt beneath a close-fitting black jerkin, it's high Napoleonic collar rising above his sideburns (I was to be told later that he changed three times before finally deciding on that outfit). He greeted each Beatle and their manager with a handshake and a pat on the arm before introducing his bride-to-be along with his bodyguards' wives. Priscilla Beaulieu was pure Hollywood starlet: her black bouffant towered above her forehead and she was heavily made up with thick black mascara, midnight blue eyeliner, red blusher and what I chose to describe as Heartbreak Pink lipstick. She was wearing a figure-hugging, sequined mini dress, black-seamed stockings, and high heel shoes.

As an entry in my precious recovered notebook reminds me, John attempted to introduce some Lennon humour into the moment by addressing Elvis in a Peter Sellers/Inspector Clouseau accent. Elvis shot me a puzzled glance but the biggest star in the world never stopped smiling. Gesturing his guests to take their seats he pointed to a table groaning with party food: 'Help yourselves if you're hungry.' It was after 10pm, however, and Paul politely told him we had all eaten. Nobody was here for the food. Instrumental music was coming from a juke box in the corner. A television was switched on but the sound was off.

What does one say at a rock summit of this proportion? None of us seemed to know. Paul made some complimentary remarks about the house which Elvis responded to pointing out that in the daytime they would have been able to enjoy a view from the rear window (more of a glass wall) 'right across the golf course – not that I play, you understand'.

Next, Elvis picked up a gadget to switch channels on the still-silent TV. George was to remind me later that it was the first time any of us had seen a remote control – back home we were still getting used to colour television.

'I hear you guys had a little trouble on the plane ride to Portland,' said Elvis slipping more comfortably into his role of host.

'Yeah, like one of the engines caught fire,' replied George. 'But I've known worse. Another time, when we were flying out from Liverpool, the window next to me blew in.'

'I took off from Atlanta once,' recalled Elvis. 'The plane only had two engines and one of them failed. Boy, I was really scared. That time I thought my number was up. We had to take out pens and things – any sharp objects from our pockets and rest our heads on pillows between our knees. When we landed, the pilot was wringing wet with sweat even though it was snowin'.'

'Yeah, we've had some crazy experiences on tour,' interjected Paul. 'Once a guy ran on stage, pulled the leads out of the amplifiers and said to me, "One move and you're dead!"'

'It can be pretty scarin' sometimes,' said Elvis clearly doing his best to make Epstein's boys feel they'd all been friends for years. 'I remember once in Vancouver, we'd only done a number or two when some of the fans rushed the stage. It was lucky the band and I got off in time – they tipped the whole damn rostrum over.'

'I suppose it's easier for us,' said John. 'When the fans went for you, you were up there all alone. With us, it's four against everybody and we can at least draw support from each other.'

The banter went on until Elvis, shifting uncomfortably in his seat, said: 'But enough of that near-disaster stuff, we're all alive and well – and here. I thought we'd sit and talk about music. You guys up for a jam session?' Four mop-topped heads nodded affirmatively and someone went to fetch the instruments he'd assembled for the occasion.

While the electric guitars were produced and plugged into amplifiers scattered around the room and a white piano was pushed into view, Colonel Parker bellowed from behind a hurriedly assembled roulette wheel table: 'Ladeez and gentlemen, the casino's open. Anyone who doesn't play a musical instrument is welcome.' Brian needed no further encouragement: gambling had become his thing. Roadies Aspinall and Evans and one or two members of the Memphis Mafia had moved to the cocktail bar for drinks and tough-guy talk and while others moved towards the latest Parker operation, I stayed close to the music – this was a session I would one day be able to tell my grandchildren about and I wasn't going to miss a single note.

Elvis picked up the bass guitar he'd been learning to play, John and George began tuning the two rhythm guitars and Paul sat down at the piano. 'Sorry there's no drum kit Ringo, we left that back in Memphis.' 'No worries,' responded the drummer, 'I'd rather play pool.' And with that he joined Jerry Schilling and Sonny West at the pool table.

It was beginning to look, and sound, like a party.

While they sorted songs they all knew, Elvis played a few notes on his bass and addressed himself to Paul: 'Still not good huh… but I'm practicing.'

'Elvis lad,' replied Paul, 'you're coming along well. Keep up the rehearsals and Mr Epstein over there will make you a star.' I shot a nervous glance at the Colonel, but with a cigar shoved into one side of his mouth and a fistful of dollars in his grip,' he hadn't heard the remark although Brian had and pulled a face. Phew! That was close.

And so Sergeant Presley's Lonesome Heartbreak Band was ready to play. In front of a privileged audience of just a couple of dozen people, a billion dollars' worth of talent was lined up to give its one and only performance.

'What's it gonna be?' asked Elvis.

'Let's do one by the other Cilla – Cilla Black,' said Paul, leading into '*You're My World*'.

'This beats talking, doesn't it,' said John. He could never resist making some obscure or barbed comment just when things were going well.

The Bel Air All-Stars proved to be just as good as one might have expected, slipping easily and freely into their individual roles. Elvis's voice rose, richer, deeper and more powerful than the others, his left leg pumping in time to the beat. You could feel the magic and he did it so naturally. Paul, on the piano, joined Elvis in some vocal duets, George worked in some of his neat little riffs and John, even if he was just going through the motions, didn't let the side down. I started to relax a bit and enjoy the piece of music history being enacted in front of my eyes.

Simultaneously, the roulette game proceeded and Ringo shot pool surrounded by six excited children while the wives and girlfriends watched the jam session with rapt expressions. Each time there was a lull, I slipped off to the bathroom to scribble the notes the Colonel had forbidden me to make but knew perfectly well I would.

Elvis was getting into the spirit of the evening. 'This is what you guys gave me for my thirtieth birthday,' he said. 'It made me sick.' Then he laughed as he led them on bass guitar into *I Feel Fine*.

'Why have you dropped the old stuff? The rock?' asked John, for once with feeling. 'I loved the old Sun records.'

For a moment, Elvis looked uncomfortable. This was one line of questioning he must have expected but clearly had not looked forward to. 'It's true I'm stuck with some movie soundtracks but that doesn't mean I can't do rock'n'roll anymore,' he said perhaps a little testily. 'I'd love one day to go back on the road just like you all are doing.' And in the only reference I heard him make alluding to matters financial, he added: 'Plus I have to put food on the table, just like you. A lot of tables…' His voice trailed off as he looked across at his gambling manager, a sad expression on his face.

John caught the change of mood and in a bid to swing it back, reverted to his Clouseau accent: 'Zis is ze way it should be… Ze small homely gathering wiz a few friends and a leetle muzic.' Elvis shook his head.

The next couple of hours slipped by and I felt I could relax even though Elvis – no fool him – asked me on one of my returns from a note-taking session in the bathroom, 'Somethin' wrong with your bladder?'

It was well after midnight when *it* happened: John on a stroll around the house once the music making had stalled, spotted an illuminated table lamp. It was made in the style of a western waggon, just like the ones the Colonel had presented to us on his gift dispatching visit to the Beatles the previous year. This one, however, was different: emblazoned on its canvas cover was the slogan, in bold capital letters, ALL THE WAY WITH LBJ. Sadly, it was the flame which lit a fire set to burn inside him for the rest of his days.

To John, Lyndon Baines Johnson was nothing less than a warmonger responsible for the slaughter of innocent civilians in what he - John - regarded as a civil war between the Vietnamese people. John's mood could change in an instant, and that is exactly what happened at the party Elvis Presley threw for the Beatles that night.

He reacted a little later when he heard Elvis, answering a question from George, say: 'Making movies gives me a lot of free time. We finished one – I won't say which – that took just fifteen days to complete.'

'Well, we've got an hour to spare now,' said the Beatle with the shark-infested mouth. 'Let's make an epic together.' To some it might have sounded like a joke but now he was clearly seething inside.

Elvis looked stunned, but held his tongue. John had been too clever to mention Vietnam outright, knowing that this would only lead to a political argument in which he would be hopelessly outnumbered. His technique in situations like this was to make people look foolish over something they believed in. By putting Elvis down over his movies, he was also belittling the King's support for the Vietnam War.

In hindsight, I would classify that crack from John as the final insult, the one that started the feud for real. Before that, the disputed territory between Elvis and the Beatles had been about record sales in the marketplace, public acclaim at the box office and headlines in newspapers. Now it would become a highly personal conflict, which had nothing whatever to do with music but everything to do with politics: a stand-off between Elvis, the staunch American patriot, and John, the vehement anti-war protester.

The former tank corps sergeant got up from the couch and went over to Sonny West and Alan Fortas, a former football player known as Hog Ears. Only Elvis and the Memphis Mafia dared call him that. He was clearly disturbed but far too polite to say what was going on in his head. I learned later that he told his pals he thought John was stoned which was quite probably true.

The atmosphere now was strained. Had I been looking for a sensational 'feud' story then I was surely on the brink of one now, but that had never been the intention. I had merely wanted to set up a meeting between the greatest music stars on Earth and cover it so that their fans could read about it in years to come. Had Brian Epstein and I thought it through we might have realised that John might misbehave. As it was, the mood he was in made his anger about America's actions in south east Asia overcome his love of rock'n'roll.

For the rest of the night – and we stayed at Perugia Way until around 2am – the hosts did what they could to put their guests at their ease. Elvis, no fool, chided me again about my frequent visits to his bathroom – he'd spotted the notebook. Having won on the tables, Parker promised to buy Epstein a cocktail cabinet 'Because I can see you like your drink', and the latter said he would have a Shetland pony dispatched to California 'to remind you of your circus days, Colonel'.

Ringo told Elvis he would be welcome to enjoy their hospitality if he cared to call over to Benedict Canyon the following day. He didn't take up the offer and he never spoke to John again.

As we stepped out into the Bel Air night, the Colonel said to me: 'Tell the fans it was a great meeting.' John overheard him and said something to the contrary.

The happiest note was struck by chauffeur Alf Bicknell: 'He called me "sir",' he said almost crying with delight. 'Elvis Presley called me "sir"!'

In what I suspect was a display of conscience, John announced the following day: 'There's only person in the United States of America that we ever wanted to meet – not that he wanted to meet us! – and we met him last night. We can't tell you how we felt. We just idolised him so much. The only person we wanted to meet in the USA was Elvis Presley. We can't tell you what a thrill that was.'

Not long after Elvis too made a statement about how he felt about them following their meeting. It included this: 'People have said my absence from personal appearances has given the Beatles their big opportunities. I know nothing about that. As for the Beatles, all I can say is – more power to them. I have watched all their television appearances over here. I don't think I should say what I feel about them. It wouldn't be fair to fellow entertainers.

'I will say the Beatles have got what it takes and in great abundance and that they've been given a heck of a vote of confidence. I'm sorry, but I have to be diplomatic and I'm honest about it. They are entertainers like myself and I guess they're as dedicated as the rest of us. Which, in the long run, is all that matters. I wish them luck.'

* * *

SHORTLY after the Beatles' return from the US, both John and Elvis lapsed into periods of melancholy. John mooched around the grounds of Kenwood with no particular place to go. He knew he had to write some songs in time for the release that Christmas of the Beatles' next album, *Rubber Soul*, but the muse had deserted him. 'I'd actually stopped trying to think of anything. Nothing would come. I went for a lie-down, having given up. Then I thought of myself as a nowhere man, sitting in his nowhere land – and that was it.'

The song that had come to him in the depths of torpor was to provide the group with yet another global hit. It was the very first Beatles song to be totally unrelated to romance or love – he now had other things on his mind. Paul was to say of his friend's composition: 'That was John after a night out, withdrawn and coming up. I think at that point he was a bit... wondering where he was going and in truth, so was I. I was starting to worry about him.'

On the other side of the Atlantic, Elvis also took frequent lone walks in the grounds of his mansion. Priscilla recalled finding him soon after the Lennon experience gazing down the escarpment of the Bel Air Country Club where a sprinkler was in operation. 'Can you see him Sattnin' (his nickname for her)?' He asked. 'See what honey, the water?' 'The angels out there? Angels.'

'I have to go baby. They're calling me. They want to tell me something.'

Elvis started to walk down towards 'the angels' on the lawn and had to be gently led back to the safety of his house.

Two rich and highly successful men living in their nowhere lands, both mentally bruised by their face-to-face encounter.

Sometime after we returned to the UK I received a message from John via a secretary at Epstein's office. The gist of it was that he thanked me for keeping my promise to arrange a meeting with Elvis Presley, he hoped he had not spoiled the occasion with his behaviour. He had apparently been in a bad mood following an argument earlier in the evening with another Beatle. He never said which.

Colonel Parker died on January 21 1997. He had been living out his retirement in a gated estate in Las Vegas, the rent paid by the owners of the International Hotel where he had gambled away most of his fortune. He had been accused of acting in collusion with RCA against Presley's best interest, of 'self-dealing and overreaching and violating his duty to both Elvis and to the Presley estate'.

10

DOUBLE TROUBLE

IF getting the Beatles together with Elvis Presley failed to have the fine results I hoped for (had they got on better they might have done a television show or even recorded together) then introducing Brian Epstein to Colonel Parker was at least to pay dividends. There came a time when the older man's experience proved invaluable for the younger at a time of major crisis for the group.

Just ahead of their 1966 US tour, the American teen magazine *Datebook* reproduced an article the writer Maureen Cleave had composed for the *Evening Standard* in London five months earlier. In an interview he had given her at Kenwood, John remarked that the Beatles were 'more popular than Jesus'. The quote had gone virtually unnoticed when the *Standard* printed it but when *Datebook* published the full interview with the seemingly blasphemous one-liner, 'Bigger than Jesus' splashed across the front cover, angry reactions flared up in Christian communities all over America.

John's faux pas was flashed across the nation like news of a major catastrophe. Promoters who had booked the Beatles to appear in stadiums across America were bombarded with protest calls. Tickets remained unsold; cancellations were rising on a daily basis. The office of Nat Weiss, Epstein's friend and New York lawyer, received dozens of complaints, mainly from the Bible Belt, warning that John would not go unpunished for his sacrilege. More than thirty radio stations announced that they had banned Beatle records. Even those dubious defenders of the faith, the Klu Klux Klan, were marching to the crackle of Beatle records burning on bonfires.

Although he was still recovering from glandular fever, Brian left his sickbed to fly to New York in a desperate attempt to salvage the tour. He evaded questions fired by journalists awaiting his arrival at Kennedy Airport only by promising to give a full-scale press conference at his hotel, the Sheraton, the following day.

These were, he said, his worst hours in the whole time he managed the Beatles. He struggled to point out to the hungry press pack which confronted him that what John had actually said was: 'Christianity will go. It will vanish and shrink. I needn't argue about that; I'm right and I will be proved right. We're more popular than Jesus now. I don't know which will go first, rock'n'roll or Christianity. Jesus was all right but his disciples were thick and ordinary. It's them twisting it that ruins it for me.'

The clarification did little to improve the situation and at that point he turned to Colonel Parker. Following their initial skirmishes, Brian frequently called him for help. Sometimes the Colonel offered his advice whether the Englishman had sought it or not. The Colonel was evasive on this point when I asked him who had placed the call, late on the afternoon (Pacific Time) of 6 August 1966, during what were probably the Beatles' darkest hours – Brian Epstein or himself? Not that it really mattered. The distressed tone that was usual in Brian's voice in such situations had been the memorable thing. An avid news-watcher, particularly when a story concerned other entertainers, the Colonel was well aware of the big trouble the Beatles were in.

Brian admitted to me later that he had been 'tense, a little frightened even', as he discussed with the Colonel the best strategy to employ with the now-hostile media. The older man hardly needed to remind him of the advice he had already given him on several previous occasions: that the Beatles should not give interviews in which they confided their private, innermost thoughts. 'You have to think of the fans, Brian,' he had said. 'The fans don't want their idols mixed up in controversy.'

'Controversy' was an understatement for the situation facing Brian. The pop manager was about to become Daniel in the lions' den. His intelligence sources delivered bleak news from all fronts.

'Tell John to apologise,' advised the Colonel.

'He refuses to apologise for something he didn't say.'

'What are you planning to do?'

'I'll cancel the tour if necessary.'

'That'll cost you plenty.'

'I've already checked and I've been told it will cost us at least a million dollars, but I don't care. I'm not going to put the boys' lives at risk even if it costs $10 million. This is developing into a holy war and I'll cancel... unless...'

'Unless what, Brian?'

During his transatlantic flight, Brian had feverishly examined his options, and he now ran one possibility past the Colonel. It had not escaped Brian's attention that the centre of the most fanatical anti-Beatle activity was Memphis, Elvis's home town and the so-called 'buckle on the Bible Belt'. Even now, Memphis city council was meeting to discuss a possible ban on the group's concert because of the Jesus remark.

Brian now wondered aloud whether Elvis, a devout (if prodigal) Christian, might be prepared to help out. Perhaps he could issue a statement saying that John's quote had been misunderstood, that he had said 'more popular than Jesus', not 'bigger than Jesus', and was really a good chap: a God-fearing Beatle.

By this time, nothing fazed the Colonel. He was used to being asked to lend Elvis's support for one purpose or another. And he was used to saying 'no'. On this occasion, however, he saw an opportunity to test his rival's mettle. It was Epstein's winding-up remark he found irresistible: 'And needless to say, if there is anything we could ever do for you…'

The Colonel must have smiled to himself. He so admired titles and the honours that invariably went with them (so much so that he had bestowed one on himself even before two obliging governors, in Tennessee and Louisiana, had seen fit to nominally approve it). He had been greatly impressed the previous year to read that the Queen had presented the Beatles with medals at Buckingham Palace. He believed that the Beatles' MBEs had been cleverly engineered through Brian's contacts in English society, soon after Brian had struck up a close friendship with the Queen's sister, Princess Margaret.

Now it was the Colonel's turn to wonder aloud. Perhaps somebody could suggest to Her Majesty that an honorary award for Elvis might be in order. It would be Britain's way of showing its appreciation for such a fine, upstanding and much-loved American. If Lennon were to be honoured by the monarch, why not Sir Elvis Presley? The Snowmen's League – Parker's 'club' for people he bamboozled – was in session and the Colonel was in the chair.

Close to desperation, Brian did his best to explain that he really had had no hand in the Beatles' royal honour: 'These things are worked out between the prime minister and the monarch,' he told Parker. 'You just can't negotiate them in the way it might be possible to swing a show business award.'

By now, Brian was convinced that the old showman was playing games with him. He couldn't seriously believe that he could pull strings to get Elvis an honorary knighthood. Or did he? The Colonel had performed the seemingly impossible on so many occasions and now here he was challenging his rival to do the same. Their conversation ended in stalemate.

Brian's next call that night was to John Lennon. Whether or not he told him about Parker's ludicrous proposition I know not, but something shifted the Beatle's previously intransigent position. His most stubborn client agreed to make a conciliatory statement to the press.

'I'm not anti-God, anti-Christ or anti-religion,' John announced soon after the Beatles reached Chicago. 'I was not saying we're greater or better. I believe in God, but not as an old man in the sky. I used "Beatles" because it was easier for me to talk about Beatles. I'm sorry I said it really. I apologise if that will make you happy.'

The tour went ahead, only for the Beatles to be unnerved by an anonymous death threat, saying that they would be shot in Memphis. There were some tense moments when firecrackers exploded at the Mid-South Coliseum during the concert, but apart from that, the tour went off without a hitch and Brian Epstein saved himself a million dollars.

It was to be the end of touring for the world's most famous band, though. After the group gave their final concert at Candlestick Park, San Francisco, on 29 August 1966, George declared he'd had enough and said he was going to quit. The others knew he meant it and reached an agreement which kept him from leaving: from now on the Beatles would be a studio group only. Their touring days were over.

In a recently discovered interview with the Canadian Broadcasting Corporation in 1969, John explained his 'bigger than Jesus' remark thus: 'It's just an expression meaning the Beatles seem to me to have more influence over youth than Christ. Now I wasn't saying that was a good idea, 'cos I'm one of Christ's biggest fans. And if I can turn the focus on the Beatles on to Christ's message, then that's what we're here to do."

11

FALLING TO PIECES

JUST as he had drawn an image of Stuart Sutcliffe on that postcard he sent me in 1965, so John Lennon insisted that the Beatle co-founder should be represented on what is probably the greatest album the group ever made: *Sgt Pepper's Lonely Hearts Club Band*. It was not, however, Sutcliffe's face on the sleeve which attracted Elvis's attention when the album was released in the summer of 1967.

For hours Presley concentrated on the song lyrics, trying to detect any anti-American or coded messages about drugs. When he came to *Lucy in the Sky with Diamonds* he believed he had hit the jackpot for the song contained just such a reference (to LSD) in its title. John had actually borrowed the line from his young son Julian, who said it was the theme of a painting he had drawn at nursery school, but to Elvis, the *Sgt Pepper* song provided positive proof that what he had suspected all along was correct. The Beatles, now shaggier than ever with large drooping moustaches, were the bellwethers of America's great unwashed druggie flock.

This was a difficult time for Elvis. The Colonel, it is widely believed, had decided that marriage would be a good career move for his client and had arranged a secret wedding ceremony in Las Vegas. Elvis married Priscilla at the Aladdin Hotel on May 1, squeezing his nuptials and the briefest of honeymoons in between filming scenes for Clambake. His friend the disc jockey George Klein, however, believes that it was Elvis's idea all along and that the Colonel did not apply any pressure on him.

'I was one of fourteen people in the room – I was a groomsman,' said George. 'Elvis had called me from California on 4 March to tell me that he was going to get married. There I was, sitting on one of the greatest secrets in show business of all time.

'The weekend of the wedding, I flew out to LA and then to Palm Springs in the Lear Jet that Elvis had chartered. It was me and Elvis, Priscilla, and Joe Esposito and his wife Joanie. We flew from Palm Springs to Vegas and the rest of the wedding party followed in another plane. We got into Vegas late at night, maybe two or three o'clock in the morning, and

Elvis and Joe went to the registrar to get the wedding licence. It's open all night long and actually Elvis went down there at 4am so that they wouldn't be crowded. We got about three hours' sleep and they had the wedding about ten o'clock in the morning. After the ceremony, we went downstairs to a reception, where the rest of the party were waiting.

'Elvis got married because he was in love with Priscilla. They had been dating for a long time, and he felt that it was the right time. He also wanted a family. I don't think the Colonel had anything to do with it; that's a misconception.'

The last thing that Elvis wanted as a wedding present was yet another collection of soar away Beatle hits, but that is precisely what he got: the group's greatest-ever creative masterpiece. *Sgt Pepper* was a tour de force so dazzling in its musical concept and so brilliant in its technical execution that it would revolutionize popular music.

The *Sgt Pepper* album also provided convincing evidence of a subtle change in the Beatles' attitude towards Elvis. It was Paul's idea to feature dozens of celebrities, both living and dead, on the most famous record cover of all time.

'We want all our heroes together here,' he said. 'If we believe this is a very special album for us, we should have a lot of people who are special to us on the sleeve with us.'

Each of the Beatles was asked to submit a list of twelve favourite heroes and heroines from throughout the ages for a tableau to be created by the artist Peter Blake and photographed by Michael Cooper. When the lists were handed in, one obvious name was missing – that of Elvis Presley.

So Stu Sutcliffe was there, along with Bob Dylan and Dion from the pop world, Marilyn Monroe, Mae West and Diana Dors (but not Jayne Mansfield), Tony Curtis, Marlon Brando and Lawrence of Arabia (ironically three of Elvis's own heroes) and W. C. Fields,

Marlene Dietrich, Carl Jung, Edgar Allen Poe and Fred Astaire. Oh, and Albert Einstein. Two of John's candidates, Adolf Hitler and Jesus Christ, were ruled ineligible on the grounds of taste.

Elvis noted the omission of his own face as he scoured the line-up searching for incriminating clues. The face that attracted his eagle eye was the bearded, patrician figure of

Karl Marx, practically the godhead of Communism, who was standing between Oliver Hardy and H. G. Wells. If anyone had doubted that the Beatles were Reds, here was the proof. In the United States, *Sgt Pepper* sold more than 2.5 million copies in three months and won four Grammy awards, further confirmation in Elvis's eyes that American youth was being held in dangerous thrall.

Brian Epstein took the unusual step of holding a special press launch party for *Sgt Pepper* at his London house at 24 Chapel Street, Belgravia, on 19 May 1967. The more I saw of him, the more I understood why the Beatles – and Paul in particular – were concerned about the state of his mental health. He and I dined frequently at Overton's restaurant in St James's. He would pore over the menu, carefully choosing his dish of the evening and instructing how he wanted his vegetables cooked or his salad prepared. He would then pop a handful of pills, insisting that I join him in enjoying what he called 'our little helpers'. The uppers were, of course, appetite suppressants, and by the time the food arrived, neither of us wanted to eat. Time after time, the lobster and fillet steak dishes would be sent back to the kitchen with 'Mr

Epstein's compliments to the chef', but never an explanation as to why they had barely been touched.

On just such an evening, he explained his absence over a prolonged period: he had been detoxed in an expensive west London treatment centre. 'I've been in the Priory getting over a slight problem,' he confided. 'You see that chap over by the door? He's my bodyguard. He's supposed to protect me from myself, if you've ever heard such nonsense. Anyway, he doesn't let me get any blues (purple hearts).'

Bidding me goodnight, he said: 'I'm off to a party where I know they'll have lots and lots of little goodies. I do hope my shadow doesn't get too tired.'

In the event, that is exactly what did happen. Brian stayed awake for three days and three nights, a feat his bodyguard could not match. The protector finally dropped from exhaustion at Brian's country house at Kingsley Hill in Sussex. The manager gave him the slip and made his way back to Chapel Street. Inside his house there, he indulged himself until his heart could take no more.

On 27 August 1967, the butler knocked on his bedroom door but failed to get a reply. The door was broken down and Brian was found dead. He was laying on a single bed, dressed in pyjamas, some correspondence he had been reading spread out over a second, unoccupied single bed beside him. Police found seventeen bottles of pills by the beds, two in a briefcase and eight in the bathroom. Death had been caused by bromide poisoning due to 'an incautious self-overdose' of a prescribed drug called Carbrital.

The news reached the Beatles in the Welsh seaside resort of Bangor, where they had gone to be indoctrinated in the art of transcendental meditation. Pattie Harrison had met the Maharishi Mahesh Yogi after a lecture on spiritual regeneration at Caxton Hall and had fallen under his spell. She had told George about the power of Indian mysticism and he had converted the other Beatles, who had become interested enough to go on a spiritual retreat that weekend.

Their lack of public reaction to Brian's death owed as much to the teachings of the Maharishi, who assured them that death was simply part of the process of reincarnation, as it did to the fact that they knew Brian had previously tried twice before to commit suicide because of what they understood to be clinical depression. Despite his success in creating things, as a businessman he was a massive failure and the sudden fortune he had amassed disappeared just as quickly.

A message bearing Elvis's name arrived in the Welsh resort, expressing 'deepest condolences on the loss of a good friend to you and all of us'. There were no prizes for guessing who had really sent it.

John was grief-stricken, although he appeared blissed out in the company of his giggling guru. Cynical though he might be, he had a very soft spot for Brian, whom he regarded as a protected species. Not only was Brian one of the few people safe from the Lennon lemon acid, John didn't like anyone else putting Brian down and that included the other Beatles.

As 'the Liverpool Lip' John was the most cutting person I ever met, even with royalty. He didn't like Princess Margaret because of her airs and graces, although he knew that Brian adored her. It had been Margaret who said that 'MBE' stood for 'Mr Brian Epstein'. In response, John changed her name to 'Priceless Margarine'. He told me about a time when he thought he had heard the Queen's sister remark that Beatle fans had inconvenienced her arrival at a cocktail party.

'I said I didn't know why she had bothered to turn up if our bloody fans were a nuisance to her,' he said. 'I didn't say it to her directly, but I'm sure she overheard me. I just hope I hadn't misheard her!'

John had to go along with the Establishment for the sake of the group, but he would rather have been one of the Stones, whom Andrew Oldham had groomed to be as anarchic as they liked. However, when John and Andrew did get together, weird things started happening.

'The Stones were still dying in the North so I decided to go and see the Beatles, the opposition, playing in Liverpool,' Andrew told me. 'After the show, I had the pleasure of being driven back to London in John's psychedelic Rolls-Royce. I'm not saying we weren't on acid and I'm not saying we were. I was high on the event, anyway, because it was a welcome home concert after they conquered America. Somehow, we got into hysterics about what would happen if the car windows suddenly shattered. John said, "It would be great – we'd have to wear the bear suits." It would be interesting to analyse that statement to find out what he meant.

'I later tried to buy that Roller from John because I believed it had two sets of windows. I was just so stoned that I hadn't realised that the windows were shut at one stage of the journey and open at another.'

The horrors that spanned the whole of the 'decade of love' were not by any means over as we were to discover.

Details began to emerge of a weird sect called 'The Family', the members of which took LSD and other drugs, practised Satanism and listened to Beatle records. Their leader, a drifter called Charles Manson, who had dubbed himself 'Jesus Christ', recruited young dropouts from the streets and took them to a desert hideout, where they were blooded in crude techniques of assassination. By December, Manson and three young women disciples had been arrested and charged with the murders of six people including the actress Sharon Tate.

When the Manson trial began in June 1970, it was claimed that the bearded, long-haired hippie had been motivated by the lyrics of *Helter Skelter*, one of the tracks on the Beatles' White album. The prosecution believed there was a definite link between the murders and the Beatles' music. Manson, himself a songwriter, proclaimed that the Beatles were prophets who, through the words of *Helter Skelter*, were predicting the outbreak of a race war in the United States.

He interpreted the title as meaning 'Armageddon'. According to Manson, when *Helter Skelter* came, the Black Panthers – led by Rocky Raccoon (the name of another track on the White album) – would rise and kill the Piggies (the title of a third track). Manson said he saw the Beatles' songs as a signal to start the slaughter.

Asked about the Manson allegations, John replied: 'Well, he's barmy. He's like any other Beatles fan who reads mysticism into it. I don't know what *Helter Skelter* has to do with knifing somebody.'

In fact, it had been Paul McCartney who had penned the words to *Helter Skelter*, about an innocent fairground ride. *Piggies*, which Manson saw as an incitement to murder members of the White Establishment, was actually a George Harrison composition and the line, 'What they need is a damn good whacking', came from something his mother had once said.

But the notion that the Beatles were more dangerous than ever stuck in Elvis's mind. It was at this point that he was personally involved in a double threat of kidnapping and assassination. Inside Elvis, something snapped.

He had only a few more nights to run of his third successful season in Las Vegas when a security officer at the International Hotel received a telephone call. The date was 26 August 1970. The anonymous male caller claimed that criminals known to him were planning to kidnap Elvis and hold him to ransom. The caller said that he had been approached to take part in the conspiracy, but had opted out.

Kidnapping being a Federal offence, the Las Vegas Police Department immediately contacted the FBI. Barely had the agency started to act on the first call when a second one was received the following day when I was visiting the Colonel in his office on the fourth floor of the hotel.

This call came from a man with a southern accent, who advised the Colonel to treat the threat of the kidnapping as a matter of urgency. Not a man to panic, Elvis's manager did just that before regaining his usual sang-froid and guiding me into the casino to chance our luck at craps.

FBI agents were still processing this call when yet another threat arrived. This time, a caller warned that Elvis would be shot on stage. The would-be assassin was named as a woman who had tried unsuccessfully to sue Elvis over the paternity of her child.

The FBI files that I was able to examine twenty years later contain the following report:

> *Call was received at twelve noon, stating that this individual who is going to kill Presley has already departed from Los Angeles airport and has apparently made a reservation for the Saturday evening performance of Presley. The potential killer, a woman, is carrying a pistol fitted with silencer.*

The files further show that J. Edgar Hoover issued instructions that he should be kept informed about any developments.

Elvis was alternately fearful and furious about the threats. He might have prophesied his own death in a Manson-style slaying, but to be the target of two simultaneous attempts was defying even destiny. When he was told of Hoover's concern for his safety, he calmed down a bit. The great man himself was on the case. He had found a saviour.

Everywhere I went, the hotel seethed with FBI activity. Fans in Elvis T-shirts and clutching one or other of the Colonel's cuddly toys swarmed excitedly through the hotel's corridors bumping into the well-padded shoulders of men in grey suits and snap-brimmed trilbys. I could tell from the beads of sweat on Joe Esposito's brow that he was nervous. When he became fidgety, I knew he was scared. He held himself personally responsible for Elvis's safety, and things were getting out of hand.

Elvis's bodyguards, some of them specially recruited for the new crisis, were given photographic ID cards not only to identify themselves to the hotel staff and members of the public but also to enable them to recognise each other. As they were all armed to the teeth, there was a very real danger that one of the new faces might be shot by mistake for getting too close to Elvis.

Elvis refused to abandon his act, but he went on stage with a gun tucked in the back of his trouser waistband. If anyone fired at him, he intended to shoot back. As Sonny West and Jerry Schilling were stationed nearby to jump in front of Elvis at the slightest sign of trouble, this could have proved fatal. Elvis had issued other orders as well: 'If anyone gets me, kill 'em before the cops move in. I don't want anyone to become famous for shooting Elvis Presley' All the precautions worked, and Elvis closed in Las Vegas without a scratch. But his aides privately reported that he was using more drugs and his behaviour was more erratic, even on stage.

Fans were sometimes treated to a rambling version of his life story. I dropped in one night and heard this: '…Like to tell you a little about myself. I started out … in childhood. I started out when I was in high school, went into a record company one day, made a record, and when the record came out, a lot of people liked it and you could hear folks around town saying, "Is he, is he?" and "I'm going," "Am I, am I?" … whew! … Elvis deterioratin' at the Showroom Internationale in Las Vegas … Where was I? … Oh, anyway, made a record, got kinda big in my home town, few people got to know who I was, that's w-u-z, was. See? So I started down in the wuz … Aw, shucks, what I mean to tell you is I was playin' around these night clubs, alleys and things. Did that for about a year and a half, then I ran into Colonel Sanders … Parker, Parker … and he arranged to get me some [Elvis blew his nose] Kleenex … he arranged to get me … Whew, I'm tellin' you … shot to hell, this boy can't even finish a sentence straight … Anyway, there was a lot of controversy at that time about my movin' around on stage so I … cleared my throat again, looked at my watch and ring and the guy said … the guy said? … the guy said nothin' … I'm the guy! I'm telling you, you better get this together, boy, or this is gonna be the last time they let you up on a stage …'

There was a lot more of the same embarrassing nonsense. Inside the Presley camp they were blaming Elvis's loss of touch with reality on his obsession with John Lennon. Sometimes he changed or forgot the lyrics of his songs; at other times, he stumbled around the stage or fumbled with the microphone. Not once, however, did the audience lose its reverence. Some fans booked in for all sixty-odd shows a month to catch the King for better or worse.

Elvis was actually in physical pain. According to Charlie Hodge, 'Elvis often needed painkillers after his act. As everyone knows, he could be very physical in his performance, with his karate stunts and so on, and he genuinely used to pull a muscle or damage himself. He did have a high pain tolerance. When they discovered he had an eye condition called glaucoma, I went with him to see the doctor. He said it was so bad that he needed to give him a shot right there, but there was no anaesthetist available. So Elvis said, "Do it!" He grabbed the side of the chair and the doctor just gave him a shot right in the white of the eye. It came up like a tennis ball.'

To celebrate the new, live Elvis, RCA released On Stage: February 1970, a collection of songs recorded in Las Vegas, in reply to the Beatles' *Let It Be album*, their 13th – and last.

***

SUDDENLY, the most famous group in the world was history. The Beatles had been falling to pieces ever since Brian Epstein's death, but the official death knell was sounded on 31 December 1970, when Paul McCartney, who had tried to keep the band together, took out a law suit in the High Court in London to dissolve the partnership.

'I was stoned all the time and I just didn't give a damn,' admitted John, who now looked like a refugee from a hippie commune. 'Idiots rang up and said, "Yoko split the Beatles". She didn't split the Beatles. After Brian died, we collapsed. Paul took over and supposedly led us. But what is leading when we went round in circles? We broke up then. That was the disintegration.'

Both Elvis and John were showing signs of disintegrating themselves. The chains of addiction had been fitted so subtly that neither realised he was enslaved until he tried to walk away. By then it was too late.

***

THERE is no way that John, Paul, George and Ringo could have known that a few minutes after midday on Monday 21 December, their very futures in the United States were being discussed with the president in the White House Oval Office. Elvis had turned up at the gates asking for a meeting with Richard Nixon. Initially security guards and then close aides of the president were shocked, but such was his fame that Elvis's request was granted. He wanted to talk to Nixon about the boys from Liverpool who were, he considered, 'a real force for anti-American spirit'. While expressing some surprise, Nixon nodded in agreement. According to records obtained under the Freedom of Information Act, Nixon responded to the anti-Beatles tirade by indicating that those who use drugs are also those in the vanguard of anti-American protest. Violence, drug usage, dissent, protests, all seem to merge in the same group of young people.

Presley indicated to the president in a very emotional manner that he was 'on your side, sir'. Elvis kept repeating that he wanted to be helpful, that he wanted to restore some respect for the flag which was being lost. He mentioned that he was just a poor boy from Tennessee who had gotten a lot from his country, which in some way he wanted to repay. He also mentioned that he had been studying Communist brainwashing and the drug culture for more than ten years. He mentioned that he knew a great deal about the subject and was accepted by the hippies. He said he could go right into a group of young people or hippies and be accepted which he felt could be helpful to him in his drug drive. The president again indicated his concern that Presley retain his credibility.

Before the meeting ended Elvis presented Nixon with a commemorative Second World War Colt .45 pistol. He did not go away empty handed: the President gave him what he came for in the first place, a badge and credentials making him an honorary member of the Federal Bureau of Investigation's Narcotics and Dangerous Drugs wing. And, in a way, he owed it to the Beatles.

At the conclusion of the meeting, Presley again told Nixon how much he supported him, and then, in a surprising, spontaneous gesture, put his arm around the president and hugged him. (The 'surprise' was that Elvis actually broke down in tears.)

By the time Elvis was being shown to the door, the agent's badge and the appropriate paperwork were waiting in the outer office and Nixon handed them over. The speed with which they had turned up indicated that the Narcotics Bureau's decision to exclude Elvis had already been countermanded before he even set foot in the Oval Office.

On 31 December, Nixon covered his tracks in a non-committal letter, carefully avoiding mention of the Beatles, sent to Graceland:

Dear Mr Presley,

It was a pleasure to meet with you in my office recently, and I want you to know once again how much I appreciate your thoughtfulness in giving me the commemorative World War II Colt .45 pistol, encased in the handsome wooden chest. You were particularly kind to remember me with this **impressive gift, as well as your family photographs, and I** *am delighted to have them for my collection of special mementos.*

With my best wishes to you, Mrs Presley, and to your daughter, Lisa, for a happy and peaceful 1971.

Sincerely, Richard Nixon

And so it was on the very day Nixon dictated his letter to Elvis that Paul began his legal action to break up the Beatles. Meanwhile, Presley was back in Washington visiting the FBI, where he pursued his vendetta against John Lennon with all the vigour he possessed.

He had arrived with William N. Morris, a former sheriff of Shelby County. J Edgar Hoover, the legendary director of the FBI, agreed to him being conducted on a tour of the Bureau, but expressed his regrets that he would not be able to meet Elvis in person. Hoover had his doubts but, like Nixon, was prepared to use Elvis to his own advantage. He would not, however, risk any flak, which a public endorsement of Elvis might attract if things went wrong. He wanted Elvis as a spy, not a Federal agent blessed by his own hand.

Hoover, too, had been gunning for Lennon for some time, without success. He had tried to prosecute John and Yoko under interstate law for transporting obscene material – the cover of their album *Two Virgins*. The album sleeve showed them in full-frontal nude pose which Hoover considered unlawful but he had been advised by his legal office that such a charge would not succeed in court. In London, however, the drug squad had raided Ringo's flat in Montagu Square where the Lennons were staying, with the result that John was fined for possessing cannabis.

His antenna tuned to the possibilities that Elvis's co-operation presented, Hoover ordered an administration assistant to prepare a confidential report on the King's FBI visit. This report details adverse comments that Elvis had made about the Beatles to FBI officers in a private conversation after his tour of the Bureau. Through the press and his own grapevine, Elvis had kept track of John's movements since his marriage to Yoko Ono on the Rock of Gibraltar on 20 March 1969. The odd couple had spent their honeymoon staging a 'bed-in for peace' at the Hilton Hotel in Amsterdam, the drug capital of Europe. John and Yoko had posed for pictures sitting up in bed, each holding a single tulip. Signs saying 'hair peace' and 'bed peace' were displayed behind them. Heavily bearded and with his hair touching the shoulders of his neatly buttoned pyjamas, John looked like a cross between the Maharishi and Charles Manson. There was no doubt in Elvis's mind, as he surveyed the evidence, that this odious oddball he had once entertained in his home thanks to me, was dangerous.

Every one of his activities came into the category of 'unsavoury', each a calculated insult to 'the Establishment' that Elvis purported to admire. John had returned his MBE to the Queen, he had held an exhibition of erotic lithographs, which Scotland Yard had raided after complaints of obscenity, and the music he was recording with the Plastic Ono Band was full of avant-garde messages in which words such as 'peace' and 'love' were – in Hoover's opinion - used to subvert the young.

Most disturbing of all, to Elvis was that despite his pleas to the President, John and Yoko had been admitted to the United States. They had travelled to Los Angeles supposedly to undergo 'primal therapy' with Dr Arthur Janov, doubtless a front for other 'questionable activities'. Whatever gossip came Elvis's way about John, no matter how fanciful, he fed into the FBI system.

The attention that John had received from the British constabulary indicated to Elvis that the former Beatle's day of judgment might arrive much sooner than his appointed hour in 'the hereafter'. It was up to him and the FBI to close the case in the United States. The thought pleased him so much that he decided to take direct action as President Nixon's own authorised drug buster. Colonel John Burrows, as he called himself when he was in FBI mode, strapped on his guns and went looking for trouble.

***

I visited Los Angeles many times during 1971 and moved there with my family the following year. I rented Ben Gazzara's house in Holmby Hills, a colonial-style mansion that looked like a miniature Graceland. After the grass-and-acid trips of the Sixties, cocaine had become the fashionable drug. 'You have to line up to get a cubicle in Beverly Hills,' one of the cognoscenti told me.

Elvis's cronies hung out at the Luau, an Haiwaiian restaurant in Beverly Hills. At other times, I saw them at the Rainbow, a rock club/restaurant on Sunset. Dealers to the stars operated at both venues without the management's knowledge.

When famous entertainers and members of the pop world were inexplicably raided in their homes by the drug squad, the suspicion grew that someone with connections was leaking information to the authorities. It now seems fairly certain that the informer was narcotics special agent, Elvis Presley. He had both the motive and the opportunity.

John Lennon himself was never caught in any incriminating situation in the United States. In fact, the only solid piece of evidence that Hoover had against him was that he had been granted a visa to enter the country after being given a discretionary waiver against a drug conviction in Britain. When he arrived with George Harrison and his wife Pattie Boyd, a full-scale FBI alert went out.

Date: 23 April 1970

Subject: John Lennon, George Harrison, Patricia Harrison

These individuals are affiliated with the Beatles musical group and Lennon will be travelling under the name of

Chambers and the Harrisons are using the name Masters. They will remain in Los Angeles for business discussions with Capitol Records and other enterprises. They will travel to New York for further discussions. Waivers were granted by the Immigration and Naturalization Service in view of the ineligibility of these three individuals to enter the US due to their reputations in England as narcotic users.

While Lennon and the Harrisons have shown no propensity to become involved in violent anti-war demonstrations, each recipient [of this memo] should remain alert for any information of such activity on their part or for information indicating they are using narcotics. Submit any pertinent information obtained for immediate dissemination.

The FBI had a star witness to attest to John's drug-taking: the Beatle himself. Around this time, he was talking frankly about his habit. If he had known the hassle that lay ahead, he might have kept his mouth shut. 'I've always needed a drug to survive: the others, too, but I always had more,' he admitted with reckless honesty. 'I always took more pills, more of everything because I'm crazy probably. I must have had a thousand [LSD] trips. I used to just eat it all the time.'

John, George and Pattie came and went without incident, and John had applied to re-enter the US again in the summer of 1970, saying he wanted to edit a film and attend a custody hearing in New York over Yoko's daughter by her former husband, Tony Cox. He was granted a visa to enter the US until September and was then given an extension. When Hoover heard that, he exploded. The FBI files show that, from then on, John was targeted like Public Enemy No. 1.

'Every agent should remain alert for any activity on his part of a potentially illegal nature,' one memo ordered. 'Lennon is a heavy user of narcotics ... this information should be emphasized to local law enforcement agencies with regards to subject being arrested if at all possible on possession-of-narcotics charge,' said another. The Lennons were followed and harassed at every opportunity.

Fortunately, they were not without powerful friends of their own. When deportation proceedings were issued against them at Hoover's instigation, John Lindsay, the Mayor of New York, where they were living, spoke out furiously about the treatment they were receiving. In a strongly worded letter to the Immigration authorities, he said that 'a grave injustice' was being perpetrated: 'The only question which is raised against these people is that they speak with strong, critical voices on major issues of the day.'

'If this is the motive underlying the unusual and harsh action taken, then it is an attempt to silence the constitutionally protected First Amendment rights of free speech and association, and a denial of the civil liberties of these two people.' Lindsay's intervention worked. The visas were granted.

***

IF Elvis had failed as a first-time husband, John Lennon wasn't proving much more reliable the second time around. He very nearly lost Cynthia's successor in his life, Yoko Ono, when he ran away with Yoko's secretary, May Pang, for a 'lost weekend' of drugs and madness that was to last eighteen months.

When I caught up with him in Los Angeles in February 1974, John had been drinking heavily for six months. Ringo had moved into the lower half of the duplex suite that the runaways were occupying at the Beverly Wilshire, and powerful Brandy Alexanders were the favourite beverage.

'I heard about your trouble,' I said to John. 'Why don't you go back to New York and sort things out?'

'I want to go home, but Yoko won't have me,' he replied miserably. 'It was all a silly misunderstanding. I left New York looking forward to a return to the good old days. Now look at me: drunk and disorderly.'

May Pang, had originally served as John's playmate in a ménage-a-trois in Apartment 72 at the Dakota, but Yoko had soon tired of the arrangement. When John and May decamped to the West Coast, May proceeded to fall in love with him.

'How long did it take before you missed Yoko?' I asked him.

'About four days,' he said. 'I keep calling her but she won't have me back, man. Can you imagine that? She won't have me back. So I get my daily Yoko from a bottle these days.'

At midnight a few weeks later, John went to the Troubadour Club to see the Smothers Brothers, whom in his outburst to the FBI, Elvis had coupled with the Beatles as a bad influence on American youth. The brothers knew John, having appeared as guests on one of his albums.

The former Beatle turned up at the club wearing a tampon taped to his forehead. This was his first mistake. He was too loaded to tell anyone whether he was making a political statement about the role of women in society or a personal one about himself. Either way, women in the audience took offence, but that didn't stop him.

He removed the tampon and kissed May Pang passionately on the lips for the photographers, knowing that Yoko, back in New York, would see the picture in the papers. Then he and his carousing companion, the singer Harry Nilsson, started to roar drunkenly to the accompaniment of cutlery rattled against glasses and plates. When the Smothers Brothers came on for their second show, John continued to sing, pausing only briefly to shout: 'Hey, Smothers Brothers, go f*** a cow.' In case anyone had failed to recognise him, he added: 'I'm John Lennon'.

When the Smothers Brothers' manager Ken Fritz tried to reason with him, a scuffle broke out and a table was overturned. John threw punches at both Fritz and a cocktail waitress who tried to intervene. With the place in uproar, John was tossed unceremoniously out onto the street and told: 'Go home and sleep it off'. Naomi, the injured waitress, said: 'It's not the pain that hurts. It's finding out that one of your idols is a real asshole.'

John moved back to New York with Harry, leaving May to pick up the pieces in LA. They occupied rooms at the Pierre on Fifth Avenue, but although the Dakota was just across Central Park, Yoko was as far away as ever. It was only after John summoned May Pang to his side and the couple moved into a penthouse on Sutton Place at East 52nd Street that Yoko began to relent. Once she decided she wanted John back, she bombarded him with phone calls, stepping up the pressure when she heard that the couple were planning to buy a house together. In late January 1975, she called John over to the Dakota for 'treatment' to help him stop smoking; he stayed the night. When he turned up the next morning, he told a speechless May Pang: 'Yoko has allowed me to come home.' John packed his bags and scampered back inside the blackened walls of the Dakota, where the door banged firmly shut behind him.

'I was like a chicken without a head,' he said when he surfaced four months later. 'I'd be waking up in strange places, or reading about myself in the paper, doing extraordinary things, half of which I'd done and half of which I hadn't done. You can put it down to which night with which bottle.'

John and Yoko now decided to try for a child, although Yoko had already miscarried several times. After visiting an acupuncturist called Dr Hong in San Francisco, Yoko became pregnant. There was a collective sigh of relief when she gave birth to the baby on John's 35th birthday, 9 October 1975. Yoko was also obsessed with numbers, so much so that she had insisted on a Caesarean section so that her baby son and John would share the same birthday. John wanted to call the boy 'George Washington United States of America Citizen Lennon', but settled for 'Sean'. 'I feel higher than the Empire State Building,' he said, resolving to forgo his recording career to become a house-husband and look after the infant.

May Pang, who married record producer Tony Visconti in 1989, has not been forgotten by others who loved John. She remained close to Cynthia – who sadly died in April 2015 - and Julian Lennon, and Paul McCartney invited her to the memorial service for his late wife Linda.

12

FAREWELL ELVIS BEATLE

JOHN Lennon surveyed the Nutopian Embassy inside Apartment 72 at the Dakota, he was aware that, whatever else it might be, it was no Valhalla-on-the-Hudson. He and Yoko had reversed the sexual poles of yin and yang, and the result was that he had been well and truly emasculated.

Purged of the sin of his eighteen-month 'lost weekend' with May Pang, he had been happy to accept the part of house-husband, a role that placed him in a subordinate position to the fiercely ambitious and cash-conscious Yoko. Although he suffered the agonies of a flawed perfectionist, he found life easier to bear when he was not in charge. Having virtually abdicated her role as John's lover, Yoko had carved another niche for herself: he called her 'Mother'.

They had moved into the Dakota – the Colditz-style castle that John had seen from a distance on the first day of his 1973 visit to New York City. Behind its portals, he enjoyed a semblance of normality and liked to give friends the impression that he had re-joined the human race, faults and all. Walking down a West Side street in 1978, he bumped into Henri Henriod, a Swiss-born roadie-turned-entrepreneur he had known since his early rock days in Hamburg. The first thing Henri noticed was the smart, business-like three-piece suit that John was wearing and his neat haircut.

'Why didn't you give us a ring to say you were here?' John asked.

'I don't have your [phone] number.'

'I'm in the book,' John said with as much satisfaction as if he had just scored another hit single. Despite the fact that he had been obliged to use an alias, he was thrilled to be 'in the book' like any other New Yorker – albeit, as John Winston.

Knowing that Henri was a close friend of mine, John asked him to give me a message: 'Tell Crispy all is well and he can stop taking the pills.'

Henri asked him about Sean.

'He's incredible – and I should know, I'm his mum,' John replied.

'You certainly have changed,' said Henri.

'Well, of course I have. You know what it was like: the pressures, the threats. All that's gone now. Just look at me – out on my own!'

They walked unnoticed towards an art shop that John wanted to visit, two old friends chatting on a Manhattan sidewalk.

'We're buying a big farm in the West – at least I think it is,' said John. 'Yoko takes care of all the buying and selling. I just thought it would be nice to raise Sean on one of those ranches like we used to see in the Elvis movies. Funny. Yoko still calls me "Elvis Beatle" if I start drifting back into the old behaviour. She spent ages convincing me that I was John Lennon and not a Beatle or an Elvis clone. Whenever I slip back, she just calls me "Elvis Beatle", and it snaps me out of the nightmare.'

This excursion on to the streets of New York proved, however, to be an increasingly rare outing. As that year passed, John stayed for longer and longer periods inside his apartment. The Dakota became his Graceland, and, like Elvis, he chose to spend much of his time inside the permanent night of his shuttered bedroom, where the giant TV screen that helped compensate for his short-sightedness was rarely switched off. Taut as a bowstring behind closed doors and darkened windows, he resented the time that Yoko devoted to other pursuits, even if some of them were aimed at multiplying what was left of his Beatle fortune. John was obsessed with a different kind of numbers game: the business of adding up figures in his life and discovering that they came to the highest number: nine. The Dakota obliged since it was situated on the corner of Central Park West and 72nd Street: seven plus two equalling nine. The apartment was No. 72, another nine.

The mansion block was circled by a moat and surrounded on three sides by a high black iron fence, which at regular intervals sprouted the head of an ominous Neptune flanked by pairs of sea-dragons. The cavernous entrance was guarded by a doorman in a bronze sentry box inside a black wrought-iron gate, over which an Indian head was carved in stone, and circled by the digits 1-8-8-1, numbers that, John noted, made eighteen or twice nine. He firmly believed that providence had brought him to the Dakota, and its connotations of the grotesque suited his mood.

The date of Elvis's demise had not escaped the notice of the numerologist in John: 16/8/1+9+7+7, or sixteen (two eights), one eight and twenty-four, which was three eights. If sixteen and eight were added to 1977, they made 2001, the popular title of Richard Strauss's classical composition *Thus Spake Zarathustra*, which Elvis had always used to announce his presence on stage.

John remembered Jayne Mansfield's tarot reader and shuddered as he recalled the man's prediction that night the weird couple came to call. He was already hooked on the divinations of Yoko's collection of astrologers, psychics, soothsayers, sorcerers and clairvoyants, without whom she was incapable of making a journey or a business decision. John had come to believe in astrology so deeply that he would never venture far from home if Mercury were retrograde.

Like Elvis, he too had become obsessed with Jesus and the idea that he, John, was a messianic figure. After his run-in with fundamental Christianity in 1966, he had gone through a phase of actually believing that he was a reincarnation of Christ and that it was his mission to spread love and peace on earth. Yoko's practitioners in the supernatural arts had cured him of that obsession, and he was now clean-shaven and still slim but visibly older, peering through his glasses.

John had previously stopped signing autographs because, he joked, he had read somewhere that Robert Redford always refused such requests. But earlier that day, he had signed a copy of Double Fantasy for a chubby, bespectacled young man who didn't look as though he had a lot going for him. Now, as John passed him, the same young man, Mark Chapman, pumped five shots into his body. John staggered but kept going, unaware that he had been shot.

'It was so sudden ... so sudden,' said Yoko. 'I didn't realise at the time that John had been hit. He kept walking. Then he fell and I saw the blood.

When I heard the full story, I remembered John's aversion to autograph hunters from our trips to the US in the Sixties when Beatlemania rolled the King. And I thought of another thing: If Elvis had succeeded in having him banned from the United States, John Lennon would still be alive today.

As friends, fans and family descended on New York and mounted a pavement vigil outside the Dakota, Yoko announced that there would be no funeral for John but that, later in the week, she would set a time for prayers to be offered for his soul. Ringo and his new wife Barbara Bach were among those who visited Apartment 72 to pay their last respects. John's remains were taken in a body bag from the morgue to the Frank E. Campbell funeral chapel on Madison Avenue. (Eerily, Elvis's body had lain in the hospital morgue on Madison Avenue, Memphis.)

Two nights after the assassination, Doug MacDougall, the ex-FBI agent who was Sean's bodyguard, arrived at Yoko's office suite in the Dakota and placed a gift-wrapped box on a desk. 'What's that?' John's assistant Fred Seaman asked. 'That,' replied Doug, 'was once the greatest rock musician in the world.' That afternoon he had picked up John's body from the funeral parlour and driven it to the Ferncliff Mortuary crematorium where he watched as it was placed in the oven. Two hours too late, Yoko had phoned to try to hold up the cremation, stating that Sean wanted to take a last look at his daddy.

I remembered John's prediction that he would die on a day with a nine in it two months after his birthday. Although he had been shot in New York before midnight on 8 December, it was already the 9th in his hometown of Liverpool, so I guess he got it about right.

LIVING WITH THE BEATLES was the tag editor Andy Gray always put beneath my name on the many articles I wrote about them for the NME.

'Well,' one American television interviewer asked me during one of the U.S. tours, 'what is life with the Beatles like?' It was crazy, wildly exciting and, of course, a great privilege to be with them for so much of the time during the heady, history-making days of Beatlemania.

We had our arguments – especially when talking about music – but I grew extremely fond of John, Paul, George, Ringo and 'Eppy', as we travelled the world together, visited each other's homes and did our best to stay out of trouble – not always easy! In my wildest dreams I could never have imagined what lay ahead when I set out on that trip to Hamburg in 1962. I hope the reader will have shared some of the enjoyment I experienced from what I have set down on these pages.

CHRIS HUTCHINS

APRIL 2015

DIANA'S NIGHTMARE
THE FAMILY

CHRIS HUTCHINS & PETER THOMPSON

Even before Lady Diana Spencer married into the most revered family on earth, she had her suspicions that the kith and kin of Prince Charles were not all they seemed-to-be. No sooner had she become the Princess of Wales and moved into Kensington Palace than her fears were confirmed: the House of Windsor constituted a flawed dynasty. She found herself trapped in a world of scandal, deceit and treachery. Diana's Nightmare reveals the previously untold secrets Diana discovered about her royal relatives. This book exposes how intensely Charles and Camilla Parker Bowles contrived to exclude her, it reveals the Queen was angry and bitter at her family's indiscretions, how the Queen Mother's indifference was matched only by Prince Philip's blind range over Diana's determination to find her own path, what really went on between the Duke and Duchess of York and how Prince Edward witnessed Diana's tantrums at Balmoral . . . Diana's own secret life.

And much, much more . .

HARRY
THE PEOPLE'S PRINCE

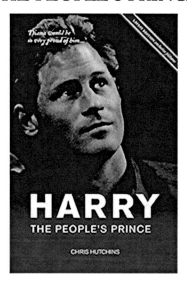

CHRIS HUTCHINS

PRINCE Harry is the most interesting – indeed the most exciting - member of the Royal Family and this no-holds-barred biography tells his story for the first time. Son of the late Princess Diana – the most famous woman on Earth – and Prince Charles, the next king, and brother of William, the king after that, he is determined to live by his mantra: 'I am what I am'. From a childhood overshadowed by his parents' troubled marriage and scarred by the tragic death of his mother, to his brilliant public performances at the Queen's Diamond Jubilee celebrations, the London Olympics and his brother's wedding, this book charts the remarkable journey of a young man with an extraordinary destiny. It also reveals details of his extraordinary love life, telling for the first time what caused his affair with Cressida Bonas to collapse. The author has enjoyed unparalleled access to a wide variety of people whose lives Harry has touched: senior aides, humble members of palace staff, aristocrats, bodyguards, school friends, comrades-in-arms . . . and old flames. They piece together the tale of a young man who admirably has created a life so different from the one set out for him by what he describes as 'an accident of birth'.

'Warm-hearted. Brave. but at times recklessly impulsive. A new biography gives a fascinating psychological insight into the forces that shaped Harry, the playboy Prince.'

Daily Mail.

FERGIE CONFIDENTIAL

CHRIS HUTCHINS & PETER THOMPSON

IT SEEMS that almost every week Sarah Ferguson - the Duchess of York, known to one and all as Fergie - makes headlines with her efforts to re-brand herself and explain her troubles. There are the weight-loss problems, the ongoing differences with the Royal Family and her financial difficulties. But how did it all start? It seemed like a fairy-tale come true when Sarah married the Queen's favourite son, Prince Andrew, and became one of the best-known women in the world. She was feted wherever she went – and she went everywhere. But the Duchess's world was to come crashing down in spectacular fashion.

We all heard the rumours, now here's a book that sets out the facts about all the scandals. Finally, the explosive truth from two experts – CHRIS HUTCHINS, the writer who broke the palace-rocking story of Fergie's risqué liaison with handsome Texan Steve Wyatt, and PETER THOMPSON, a former editor of London's *Daily Mirror*, the paper that ran the sexy St. Tropez stories of Fergie and her "financial advisor" Johnny Bryan. The book also details her often-tempestuous relationship with Princess Diana and how both women decided to end their marriages.

ATHINA
THE LAST ONASSIS

CHRIS HUTCHINS & PETER THOMPSON

BY way of light relief as Greece continues to stand face-to-face with financial meltdown, it is well worth visiting the story of Athina Onassis Roussel, who became the richest little girl in the world when she inherited unimaginable wealth from her heiress mother, Christina Onassis. This compelling book explores the legend of Athina's grandfather, the shipping magnate Aristotle Onassis, and examines the legacy that became Athina's extraordinary birthright as The Last Onassis. No 20th-century saga features more great names than that of the Onassis dynasty; the Kennedys - including JFK and his widow Jacqueline, who became Onassis's second wife - the opera diva Maria Callas who longed to be the third; and Prince Rainier and Princess Grace, with whom he fought a celebrated feud for control of Monte Carlo. The cast list is endless: the Hollywood stars Elizabeth Taylor, Richard Burton, Marilyn Monroe and Greta Garbo, the politicians Sir Winston Churchill and Richard Nixon, the tycoons Stavros Niarchos and Howard Hughes and the FBI chief J. Edgar Hoover.

ABRAMOVICH
THE BILLIONAIRE FROM NOWHERE

DOMINIC MIDGLEY AND CHRIS HUTCHINS

'An incredible story' – *Mail on Sunday*; 'Well researched and fluently written' – *The Times*; 'Draws a picture of a man of immense ruthlessness, nerve and charm . . . offers a Vanity Fair of Russian oligarchy' – *The Spectator*; A superb insight into the Chelsea boss . . . a must read for both football fans and business tycoons' – *Sunday Business Post*; 'A well-researched investigation into the life and times of Chelsea's owner' – *World Soccer*; 'The first sustained effort to uncover the making of Chelsea's oligarch' – *Guardian*; 'Authors Dominic Midgley and Chris Hutchins go to commendable lengths to tell the story' – *Sunday Times*; 'Where this book sets itself apart is in its quest to discover Abramovich's true identity. Interviews with his childhood friends, neighbours and teachers in Russia offer an original perspective on the man while access to the informed such as Boris Berezovsky, his one-time mentor, provides a picture of a canny dealmaker and consummate politician' – *The Times*; 'Most fascinating account . . . should be read by anyone not just with an interest in sport but also in business and in politics' – *Press and Journal*.